To Liz

My Pets and Other Family

by
Janet Brewster

With warm wishes,

Janet

JANET BREWSTER

Janet Brewster was born in Hampstead, grew up in North London (apart from wartime evacuation to Taunton and Newport). Worked as a legal secretary and social worker in London and overseas , whilst continuing to be a Sunday painter/ poet.

Married Doug Morrison in 1952 who worked in the Diplomatic Service and posted to the former Rhodesia (now Zimbabwe) and Malawi over a period of 15 years, apart from the 5 'apey' years spent in The Gambia.

Had a one-woman art exhibition in Malawi in 1975 and has always had a passion for painting and drawing as well as writing and poetry. At age 57 put on the backpack and travelled extensively around India. Now lives in Rottingdean, Brighton (with sanity restored).

This edition published by
Different Books Publishing 2009

ISBN: 978-0-9561410-1-9

Printed and bound by DPS Limited,
Burgess Hill, West Sussex RH11 2PD

Cover illustration Janet Brewster
Production Rachel Brown, John Witherden
and Jack Witherden

Different Books Publishing
Burgess Hill, West Sussex RH15 9AE
www.differentbooks.co.uk
A division of JWA Outsourcing Ltd

In memory of Stella Brewer OBE and Eddie Brewer OBE and their work for wildlife. And my late husband Doug for putting up with all the bites he sustained from my many pets. To Julian who is my inspiration and Jo for her encouragement.

With acknowledgement to the late Gerald Durrell whose books obviously influenced my life.

ILLUSTRATIONS

INDEX

CHAPTER 1
CAPTIVATION

He could hardly have been called handsome, his ears were far too large and he had a dent in his nose, which I had taken to be a scar. The sideburns of his jet black hair were flecked with white and this, with those tiny laughter lines around his eyes, lent a rather distinguished impression. When he expanded his massive, hairy chest and flexed his biceps, he could almost have been a Mr Universe – that is while seated – for once he stood it was impossible not to notice that nature had stunted him with the most preposterously stumpy legs.

I first saw him on the African launch 'The Ladywright' as it turned around from its up-river destination, Basse, before chugging its way back down the River Gambia to the capital, Banjul. It was not as if he even noticed me that first day as he boarded in the company of a wizened, old, African man. They settled themselves in the stern of the boat, the old man sprawling on top of some tea-chests and he sitting somewhat aloofly on the wooden slatted bench, studying his finger nails, as if engrossed in the profoundest contemplation.

An attitude I was to become only too familiar with, but never to learn what devious thoughts lurked beneath that protuberant, furrowed brow. His whole being appeared so regal and he seemed oblivious of my interest in him and the shipboard clamour that surrounded him. I wondered how he came to be travelling with such a seemingly incongruous companion, for they appeared to ignore each other. I also wondered whether they frequently made the voyage, as they appeared so disinterested in their surroundings, as if familiar to them.

The upper deck table steward came in search of me to tell me lunch was ready and to chide me for straying below-decks. As lunch was served under the comparative shade of the tattered *fo'c'sle* awning I endeavoured to find out from the steward as much as I could about the fascinating new passenger.

I discovered his name was Titan and that he had been reared by a French family up country and Titan and the man were only travelling as far as the ferry, which would take them into neighbouring Senegal to the capital Dakar.

A pang of disappointment gripped me and my appetite for the delicious looking groundnut stew placed before me, quite vanished. He would only be on board for twenty-four hours! I simply had to find out more about him, and somehow make his acquaintance.

Having only eaten a few mouthfuls of the stew, I slid away from the table, only to come face to face with the reproachful steward.

"I get belly *palaver* ." I offered by way of explanation.

I made my way down below again but it was now extremely crowded as I pushed my way through, stepping over passengers squatting on the floor. I could not see Titan until I was quite near to him. He and the old man were eating their lunch, which consisted of chunks of French bread and somewhat overripe bananas. Yet Titan ate this meagre fare with all the refinement of a gourmet savouring some speciality dish. The steward had said he had lived with a "very big boss" in French Guinea, which I took to refer to the gentleman's status rather than dimensions. Therefore, I found it easy to imagine Titan languishing in some tropical mansion, waited on hand and foot by a retinue of servants, living en famille with a distinguished French family. He probably even dressed for dinner.

When I was only a few feet away from him he looked up, his lively, rounded, hazel eyes meeting my gaze, almost with astonishment, as if I were someone he knew and had not expected to see. I felt like a star-struck teenager in the presence of her idol. I mumbled something, not really knowing what I said, at once realising he would not understand English anyway. His generous mouth spread into a reassuring smile, as if to put me at ease. He extended his hand and took mine in his firm, confident grip and I was aware of the downy black hairs on the back of his hand tickling my wrist. He lifted my hand to his lips as if to kiss it, with such old-fashioned charm, but knowing him as I later did, I realise I was probably fortunate that he had not bitten it!

Callous laughter broke out around us, derisive of such unfamiliar gallantry. The spell was broken, Titan turned away to focus his attention over the side, to stare down into the depths of the river. Dejectedly, I jostled my way back to the gangway, feeling I must have imagined that sparkle of rapport there had appeared between us. Perhaps I merely reminded him of someone he had once known. As I pulled myself up the steps, however, I felt compelled to turn and to my utter joy I discovered I still held his attention. Oh dear! Had I rushed away too soon? He looked so vulnerable and out of place, Little boy lost.

How well I came to know that pose, always guaranteed to tug at my heartstrings and ensured of forgiving him his latest misdemeanour. The pleading, helpless gaze, followed by a turned heaving back, hunched and apathetic. I never did learn to resist it. Such docile moods never lasted for long, he would soon revert to his brash, cavorting self again. His personality was so split you could almost run a rake through it! I did try to match my mood to his, but it was not humanly possible to keep pace with his every caprice.

I returned to the dubious luxury of our cabin, which had been opened up to us on boarding 'abracadabra' fashion, and presented as, 'dee President's Stateroom'. Our open-mouthed stares and gasps on entering were taken to be in awe, prompting the steward to continue to inform us how it had originally been designed for a former Governor General. It was hardly the chamber I envisaged some omnipotent, Colonial administrator conducting his affairs from, nor a President of a newly independent African State. It was cramped, dingy, hot and airless, and any former grandeur long since decayed away. There was the advantage of being able to stretch one's arm out to reach the adjacent escritoire without getting up from the lower bunk. Except when I did so, my hand encountered something warm and silky in the upper drawer, bringing me promptly to my feet. A pair of beady, brown eyes regarded me from the open drawer in an expression of horror, equalled only by my own.

What type of rat it was I did not pause to decide, shutting the drawer and abandoning my writing materials for the remainder of the cruise. It may well have been the much sought after, rare Gambian Pouched Rat, about which some zoologists really rave. I had reported it, of course, more out of a sense of duty towards the President, than by way of complaint. Several members of crew came on inspections and whilst all agreeing it was definitely a rat, did not consider it within their jurisdiction. The Health Inspector had made a visitation before leaving Banjul and since the rat had not been discovered then, it must have boarded further up-river. Which appeared to dismiss the matter to everyone's satisfaction.

The ultimate luxury of the cabin was the en suite bathroom, which steamed and gurgitated from behind a torn, stained sheet of plastic. It consisted of a cisternless, aged lavatory which emitted steam from some mystic source and leaning close to this was a tube of piping which spluttered jets of boiling water from everywhere but the nozzle and was identified as being a shower. It would have been far too hot to shower under, even if it had worked, but served as an efficient, if unnecessary, form of central heating, making the cabin more humid than the most sweltering, up-country outpost. Even in the cramped confines of the deck below, at least a little warm river air circulated.

As my eyes adjusted to the gloom of the cabin, I paused until the scuffling rodent footsteps receded into the safety of the desk drawer, and saw the sheet-enshrouded bulge on the upper bunk move. A limp arm, blotched with mosquito bites, against a background of prickly heat flopped over the side and a fever-parched voice begged for water. I was instantly ashamed of my neglect of poor Doug. Whilst I had been mooning around infatuated, my husband lay in the grips of an up-country tum. He had somehow succumbed to its agonies whilst still only a few miles out of the city, his system being particularly prone to such bugs and sensitive to changes of water. Typically, I had forgotten to bring the 4 gallon can of water he had prudently filled before departure and always travelled with. I dropped what was left of the cubes of ice I had scrounged from the cook into the jug of murky water. They instantly dissolved but must have brought the temperature down to tepid and at least appeared to dilute the browny-green colour. I turned his sweat soaked pillow but the underside seemed no drier and sponged him with a hot flannel from the furnace-like bathroom, which did little to lift his spirits. Even worse, I noticed amongst Doug's speckled blotches, some fresh, larger and redder marks. I wondered whether a rash normally accompanied up-river fever, or whether the resident rat was not the only creature to escape the

Health Inspector's attention. I felt it wiser to say nothing to him in his current, weakened state.

"What happened today?" he asked, feebly.

I had gone into the cabin each day after lunch and reported to him on the events he was missing, as mundane as they usually were. For, apart from the novelty of our first port of call out of Banjul, the remainder, like the river vegetation, were all identical and unvarying. A ramshackle wharf near a cluster of thatched houses with a bustling assortment of people, livestock and cargo. For practical reasons, in the heat the Sunday joint is transported on the hoof, or in the case of chickens, casually tied by the legs and carried upside-down. I well remember the shock when as a newcomer to Africa I was *dashed* my first chicken. I thought it had felt warm and I nearly dropped it when it started to crow!

Travelling African women appear to take all their worldly goods with them, even on short family visits and their itinerant belongings literally including the kitchen sink, or the equivalent plastic bowl. Pots and pans, bedding and clothing tied up in bundles of brightly-coloured local cloth. Not to mention sacks of rice, maize, fruit and home-grown vegetables. Not only does she raise a load that would challenge many a weight-lifter, casually onto her head, but then proceeds to traverse the rickety, swaying gangway with all the grace and poise of a Russian ballerina. In my efforts to emulate, I have never managed to take more than two steps with 'Larousse Gastronomique' balanced on my head, on wall to wall carpet at that. Although the battered appearance of the edition does tend to afford me something of a reputation as a cook! Whereas your average African lady would readily walk all day with a complete set of Encyclopaedia Britannica perched upon her head.

Mousa, a member of the crew who wore many hats, (most in fact, apart from that of the Captain whom we had never seen), had also taken on the duty of being my personal guide.

"Quick, quick! Missus" he would often call, prizing me out of a precious sliver of shade I had discovered.

"Come lookum, plent' fine animals" he would cry. "Ah! So sorry!" by the time I reached him, mopping my brow, I saw only the surfacing bubbles of what he assured me had been a recently emerged hippo.

"He get big big teeths, dis one," he would regale me, opening his mouth wide by way of demonstration, so exaggerated and descriptive were the accounts, that I could almost believe I had seen them for myself.

Opportunity to view wildlife had been somewhat limited but it only took a little imagination to visualise the troup of a hundred baboons that had just leapt into the dense interior, from the swaying, lashing foliage, left in its wake. The long, tidal streak that was surely a rapidly submerging crocodile, why I was certain I had spotted a pair of amphibious eyes. One night I had pointed out excitedly to my fellow passengers what I took to be a huge floating man-eating croc.

"Bambo" I had cried, airing my single word of *Mandinka*

"Firestick" they so derisively replied.

The only reason the word *bambo* had stuck in my mind, was the fact that in Chichewa, the language of far away Malawi, it is a respectful term of address for an old man or father. I had, therefore, found it somewhat alarming when Mousa had first pointed out a submerging *bambo*, which I fully took to be a drowning, old man, or some local, senile eccentric who dived for coins!

I proceeded to tell Doug of the current morning's activities. About a man and his sons waiting at Basse who paddled alongside in their dug-out canoe to take possession of a modern outboard motor and how, whilst endeavouring to fit it into their craft, they suddenly capsized, leaving them floundering in the water struggling to retrieve their precious new motor. There had been a young man collecting a shiny new bicycle who had ridden it experimentally around the wharf, but the front wheel slipped into a hole, throwing him over the handlebars. The old lady, bent and wrinkled, who had hobbled alongside shouting to the crew and pointing to a large iron bedstead. They tossed it over to her, somewhat haphazardly, as she beamed a toothless smile at them. She then blithely lifted the cumbersome object onto her head and staggered up the dusty track, cackling to herself.

"She was really old." I told Doug "Is there no such thing as chivalry?"

"Shivery." Doug mumbled, before rambling on something about greenfly in the nasturtiums. So I never had a chance to tell him about Titan.

When I went down to see him again that evening, I had to traverse the undulating forms of praying Muslims. They were bobbing up and down in all directions, due to a discrepancy over the river's tortuous course the precise bearings of Mecca had become difficult to ascertain. The ritual of praying was being observed more fervently than usual, due to it being the month of the Ramadan fast.

Titan rose to his feet when I neared him and greeted me almost as an old friend, and as he took my hand I could not help but consider he held it longer than politeness decreed. It was the type of clear, starry night that can only be fully appreciated in the tropics, after the fierce sun has burnt itself out. We sat in the stern together, companionably silent, watching the rippled reflections of moonlight distorted by our wake. A boisterous crowd of youths had boarded and their rowdy behaviour somehow served to draw us closer together. I felt us to be in sublime harmony and took him to be one as sensitive as myself – how wrong I was! He was more the kind that had I said,

"Oh look! What a beautiful butterfly" he would likely as not have crushed it between his great, beefy hands!

Without my having been aware of it, he had reached into my pocket and taken out a packet of cigarettes and extracting two, placed them both between his lips, flicking my lighter across them, he lit them in one smooth practised movement. Not unnaturally, I had expected him to hand one to me, instead of which he proceeded to puff away on both cigarettes frantically, like some demented, nicotine-craved addict! He certainly appeared to have unusual habits, but then I suppose, he was French.

It was just the same with the coke. I had taken down two large cans of coca-cola to quench our sun-parched thirsts. He opened them both and with one in each hand took prodigious, alternating swigs from each can.

With two coca-colas and ten cigarettes disposed of, he was decidedly enlivened and the earlier mood of repose seemed to have entirely left him. Standing on a nearby packing case, he broke into a strange sort of dance, which I took to be some form of French clog-dance. He vocalised in low staccato grunts, though whilst being untuneful, was not entirely without appeal. This soon caught the attention of those around us who were still ravenously eating their *chop* at the end of the day's fast. They began to tap their feet and give bulging-mouthed encouragement. This spurred Titan on to more daring feats of buffoonery, like tight-rope walking along the deck rail, so unsteadily, I quite expected him to topple overboard. It was only when he shinned up the mast that his companion at last stirred. Lifting his red fez, which had been tilted over his eyes, he shouted gruffly to Titan in an Afro-French Patois. In response, Titan zoomed down the mast and pounced on the frail, old man. Slapping him soundly on the shoulders and snatching the fez from his head. Balancing it on top of his own head, he swaggered up and down the deck, as if mimicking the old man. By this time, drawn by the sounds of merriment, most of the steerage passengers were crowded around us in the stern.

As if suddenly remembering my presence, Titan bounded over guffawing like a blunt hack-saw and grinning a dazzling smile. Taking my hand he tugged me to my feet, leading me into a sort of African square dance. Shedding all inhibitions, I captured his carefree spirit and when someone produced a transistor radio, everyone joined in a spontaneous *hi-life.* It was unfortunate, but immaterial that the radio was tuned in to the BBC Overseas Service, which was transmitting Rachmaninoff's Prelude in C Sharp Minor.

Life, to Titan's way of thinking, was to be enjoyed to the full and with his personal branch of *joie de vivre*, spontaneous parties were the order of the day. He was quite unable to resist an audience, he would literally stand on his head and turn cartwheels if he thought it would draw a crowd.

Sleep proved more elusive than ever on the old launch that night, the creaking hull echoing the splendour of a past Colonial era, not to mention the ravages of white ant. Doubtlessly named after some long since demised grand Governor's Lady, the 'Ladywright' soon to be scrapped, chugged her way down the same African waterway where the early explorer *Mungo Park* had perished. The prevailing clamour was maintained throughout the night, as she docked at the frequent, scheduled calls. The clangour of the anchor as it was dropped and weighed, the continuous grating of winches and conflicting orders being bellowed fore and aft. Passengers embarking and disembarking carrying on loud conversations, goats bleating as if in protest, knowing they were destined for a *Koriteh* feast and cocks crowing, mistaking the floodlights fore as being an early dawn. Even when underway, the commotion continued, as newly embarked passengers settled themselves down and I wondered if there was only the one nocturnal drummer, or whether several drummed in shifts, accompanied by a cora, a banjo-like instrument.

I doubt that I would have slept anyway, my thoughts dwelling on Titan's future. Mousa had told me that from *Dakar* he would either travel to Europe or America and I found the prospect intolerable. For one of his ebullient disposition, who had known only the freedom of a small province where he was accepted, to have to become confined and isolated in some polluted, overcrowded city, it would surely break his spirit. It did not appear that definite arrangements had yet been made. If only I were able to intervene somehow!

Having slept soundly throughout the noisy night, Doug woke up looking a little better and said he thought he would get up. He was eager to get up on deck to see where we were, for so far his view of up-country Gambia had been limited to the shafts of light that flickered through the wooden louvre door. The crew were delighted to see him recovered, and almost seemed surprised, that I wondered just how many of their tourists did actually survive! Even the large man in dungarees, who often slept outside our cabin, came up and shook his hand.

"Who is he?" Doug asked

"I don't know. I think he must be an engineer, he always wears those oily dungarees."

Everyone rallied around intent on Doug's comfort, settling him down in the prow of the vessel, one producing a footstool, another his blanket to make some shade and the electrician donated his precious old deckchair. Unfortunately, he left before we had chance to ask for instructions and the erection of it proved quite complex. It was an ornate museum piece, which I had only seen in old movies in a tropical setting or in early photos of

Somerset Maugham. As always in Africa though, there was no lack of advice and assistance, everybody considering he knew how it worked, but Mousa soon solved the puzzle, with his usual aplomb. The table steward brought Doug a cool drink and he settled down to read his book, 'Sanders of the River', which he had felt an appropriate time to re-read.

He looked really comfortable as I walked away and looked back to wave. Not that there was much of him visible, his wide rimmed bush hat pulled well over his face, buttoned up shirt with long sleeves and long trousers covering his legs. Although I have known him venture out similarly attired in the past, only to return with badly sunburned hands and a mosquito-bitten neck. He is simply one of those unfortunate people whose skin has no tolerance to ultra-violet rays and every miniature vampire in the vicinity will seek out his blood. Yet undaunted, he soldiers on, choosing to work in the diplomatic service on the Dark Continent and seeing as much of it as he can. I personally think it due to coming under the influence of Rider Haggard at an impressionable age!

Mousa accompanied me down to see Titan but he barely lifted his head in greeting. He was curled up on the seat, foetal-like with his hand clutched to his ears. I was alarmed on first seeing him, fearing he too had fallen victim to the dreaded river fever, but when he looked up, it was obvious he suffered nothing worse than a hangover. Only the first of many I was to witness, not that it was ever really his fault but people who pressed drinks upon him of mixed and varied brews. This one had apparently been palm wine, we were told that the revellery on the lower deck had gone on until the early hours, during which time, several gourdfuls had been consumed.

Titan grunted in our direction, turning over to cover his eyes and I gave his head a sympathetic stroke.

"Dis one, I *savvy* him too much." Mousa laughed. "He go make party all dee time." He shook his head in admiration.

"What is going to happen to him in *Dakar*?" I asked.

"Dis ole man, he go sell him" he replied.

"Sell him!" I screamed, shocked that such trade still existed, I fully thought there were laws against that sort of thing, but then this was Sene-Gambia, the bygone nefarious slave-trading coast.

"Er. Em. How much for?" I ventured to ask.

"Oh, plent' money. I *savvy* dee white man like Titan too much. Maybe £100" he proferred. A hundred pounds in 1968 was a great deal of money.

"A hundred!" I mouthed despondently, contemplating the £40 currently burning a hole in my bank account – but what was I thinking of, it was not as if I could be party to such barbarity. I had always despised the trade and condemned those who perpetuated it.

The old trader began to stir and gather together their bundles with all the vigour of one who has recently partaken of an excess of palm wine. Panic began to seize me as he roughly shook Titan by the shoulder beckoning him to follow. We were nearing the Farafenny Ferry.

"Ask him how much he would take." I blurted, all reason lost, panic setting in.

Mousa shouted to the man, calling him and Titan over and after a few disinterested responses, he slowly approached. There then ensued what seemed an interminable discourse in *Wolof*, whilst I shot my gaze from one to the other, endeavouring to glean the trend of the conversation from tone and expressions. Never an easy task, African languages being made up of monosyllabic grunts emitted from somewhere in the depths of the abdomen, rather than the mouth. Then there are the protracted stipulated greetings and responses to be got through, before the subject matter may be politely introduced.

After what seemed minutes, Mousa at last turned to inform me,

"He say 125 American dollars."

Having no idea at all of the current rate of exchange of a dollar, this meant absolutely nothing to me, I asked Mousa what that would be in Gambian Sterling – The Gambia being the very last country to relinquish the old fashioned pound, shillings and pence, long after British decimalisation.

Mousa turned back to the man and an even longer discussion ensued, but this time with the benefit of the opinion of the many onlookers who had gathered, all appearing to be international financial experts. As far as I was able to gather, the problem was more the current value of the Senegalese Franc, rather than fixing a price.

I was getting into a frenzy of impatience, as the original point of the discussion appeared to have been forgotten in favour of fluctuating world currencies and Mousa and the trader contributing nothing to it. We were drawing near to Farrafenny.

"He say about £56.10.8d" Mousa at last arrived at a precise figure.

My heart sank, I dare not look at Titan, I turned to leave, mumbling more to myself than anyone else, that I only had £40.

The old trader for the first time shedding his customary languor sprang to life, bounded after me saying

"D'accord Madame."

"Savoir" I replied, being the first French word to spring to mind.

"Oui, savoir" he agreed, smiling through *kola* stained teeth.

Not being practiced in the African custom of bargaining at that time, I did not place any significance on his ready acceptance of my offer, I later realised that I should have haggled and brought him down to a considerably lower figure. However I was so relieved that I had rescued Titan, that it never crossed my mind.

I produced my cheque book and Mousa obligingly bent over for me to lean it on his back. I asked who it should be made out to, but was told 'cash' would suffice, the trader apparently having a relative that worked in the French bank.

I handed the cheque to him and he was about to leave, when I asked if I should not have some form of receipt, bill of sale or identity documents, it seemed so impersonal and even dogs had pedigrees.

The man reached into the depths of the folds of his faded blue *warrumba* and produced a creased, dust-stained envelope, which he handed to me. I felt quite pleased with my foresight in requesting it, knowing Doug sets great store on such formalities.

The crowd who had taken part in the transaction thronged around me, patting me on the back and shaking my hand, leaving me in no doubt that I had done the right thing. I became quite carried away in the overwhelming warmth of the occasion, that I felt

I should be handing out cigars. In the absence of them, I settled for handing out king-size cigarettes all round.

"Dis one, 'e neber make *humbug*, he go walk good by himself"

"He go to dee market, I see him many times, go buy t'ings."

"He clean the house, maybe cook the *chop*"

"One man teach *ndemo* ride bicycle."

"Nudder man, make him drive car."

"Dis one, neber go t'ieve."

Titan's virtues were enumerated endlessly and it appeared I should never have to lift a hand whilst this versatile character was around.

Mousa was as excited as I was and he rushed over to wake up Titan, who had dropped off to sleep again, to tell him the good news. I saw them shaking hands and slapping each other on the back, Titan catching the infectious air of bonhomie.

I asked Mousa if he could find out from the Purser what additional fare was due for Titan's continued passage, explaining that he would now naturally be travelling first class with us. Knowing it to be a further detail Doug would be sure to appreciate.

Mousa grinned, a slow knowing smile, explaining that he was also the Purser and would consult his manifest.

Titan ran over to me, flinging his arms around my neck, he covered my face with squelchy kisses – it was just as I had visualised. It was only as we made our way up to the upper deck that a twinge of doubt began to deflate my euphoria and I realised that Doug knew absolutely nothing about the existence of Titan. I wondered how I should best break the news, particularly in his current convalescent state.

I decided upon a plunging in the deep end approach, rather than some pre-rehearsed speech to prepare him. In any case, I could not see how I could possibly shake Titan off now, clinging to my back and he was bound to ask for some explanation of his presence. He always prophesed to being a fatalist – now I could put it to the test.

"How are you then dear?" I greeted him with forced cheerfulness and concern. "You certainly look comfy up here."

"Yes, I feel much better. I was just talking to...." He broke off, shook his head and blinked a few times, as if not sure whether the delirium of the previous day had entirely left him.

"What. What's that?" he tentatively asked.

"What's what, dear?" I stalled.

"That thing...... that monkey on your back?"

"Monkey? Oh you mean Titan. No, he's not a monkey, he doesn't have a prehensile tail you see." I added somewhat indignantly. "He's a chimpanzee. They call them *ndemo* in *Mandinka*. "Come and meet Doug then." I said to Titan, lowering him down.

"Ooh! Ooh! Ooh!" he emitted emphatically, jumping up and down excitedly, flicking his hands in front of him.

"See how much he likes you." I encouraged, even feeling a little peeved that his initial reaction to me had been one of total indifference.

"Oh. Hello then." Doug said to him somewhat self-consciously, in a voice men normally reserve for small babies, when uncertain just how much they will understand. My confidence grew, I felt we were getting off to a good start.

"Chimps aren't indigenous to The Gambia you know, I never expected to find one here. I knew they were in Sierre Leone and Guinea, and then of course there is the chimpanzee belt which stretches across Central Africa, Tanzania, Zaire,....."

"Who does he belong to?"

I pretended not to hear, and continued.

"Very closely related to man of course, I mean look how human his hands are, except they have an opposable thumb. Isn't Titan a dynamic name?"

"Yes, it's alright. Where does he come from?"

"Guinea, I think."

"Which Guinea?" Doug asked pedantically, being so keen on African geography.

"Oh, is there more than one? Titan means one of superhuman strength, wisdom and endowed with good looks. Aren't you my little precious?" I drawled to Titan, who had settled to plucking my eye-brows.

"Did you manage to buy a hand of bananas?" Doug asked.

“Ba-na-nas!” I exclaimed, I had quite forgotten and now it seemed I would need to purchase several hands, rather than the one Doug had hoped to take back.

I owned up to my having forgotten but said Mousa was sure to find some, like the genie he was, Mousa materialised at that moment, studying a large, tattered black book.

“That man no pay ticket for Titan” he complained. “We get no price for chimpanzee.”

“What about a dog?” I suggested

“Na.” he said, having studied Titan, “He be too much tall.”

“A goat?”

“Na, he na so big.”

We eventually compromised on the difference between the fare for a dog and a goat, deciding Titan was somewhere in the middle.

“Lookum, Titan.” Mousa said, bending down to him with a large bunch of succulent black grapes, the like of which we never saw in The Gambia.

Doug had looked up at the sight of the grapes, having taken them to be a convalescent’s treat. He looked quite crestfallen when Titan had taken them and sat relishing them one at a time, carefully extracting pips from his lower, protruding lip. Tactfully I managed to break off a cluster to give to Doug, but the glance that Titan shot at him, I felt did nothing to cement their relationship.

Having devoured the entire bunch, Titan licked his fingers, and picked up Doug’s glass of coca-cola which had been on the floor beside him.

“No, put that down!” Doug ordered in a fever parched voice.

“Ooh! Ooh! Ooh!” Titan erupted, putting the coca cola back and flailing his long arms at Doug.

“Hey, Titan, lookum.” Mousa called him away, producing the largest, most succulent looking orange we had seen since we left England. Titan set about peeling and quartering it, savouring each small section slowly, as he placed pith and pips in a neat pile beside him.

I glanced at Doug expecting to see him as impressed with Titan’s exemplary manners and awaited a nod of approval, but his drooling attention was held fastened fixedly on the orange. The expression on his face was more that normally seen on the faces of hospital patients whilst their visitors sit eating their grapes.

"Who does he belong to?" Doug asked, obviously trying to take his mind off the juicy orange, the smell of which was even beginning to make my mouth water.

"Well, er, me now actually." I ventured, braced for some horrified reaction but there was merely a prolonged, agonising silence which I was compelled to fill.

"He'll be no trouble, I know how you love animals and you've always seemed interested in chimps at the zoo. He was going to Europe for sale and I thought it might be for vivisection and I simply could not bear it. He would have felt the cold too. He's too intelligent for a zoo."

"He be my good friend long time." Mousa came to my timely rescue.

"He na make *palaver* Sir. He trained by big man. He be your *piccan*."

From Doug's dazed expression I did not somehow see him becoming a father figure to an ape.

At that point the well built man in the greasy overalls came over and shook him warmly by the hand.

"Congratulations sir" he said to Doug. "I see you are looking after my old friend here. I hope you had a pleasant passage."

"Who is that man?" I hissed at Mousa

"Why dat be our good Captain, you no *savvy* him?"

"No, I thought they always wore a cap and lots of gold braid."

People began to appear from all over the boat seeking Doug out for congratulations and singing Titan's praises, and every time we appeared with him, there would be a rousing cheer. In these circumstances, it was difficult for Doug to raise too many objections and he appeared most restrained. However, this left me feeling more uneasy than if he had bawled me out, as I was constantly speculating just how he did regard Titan. I realised it had been a gross omission on my part not to have sounded him out regarding his feelings towards chimpanzees in the past but I could not recall the subject having ever arisen. I pondered over other species I might bring up for discussion, just in case a similar situation should arise in the future.

He was obviously not as enamoured of Titan as I had been, but in the awe of that first meeting, I would probably have been prepared to believe he could read and write!

In an effort to impress, I had produced the document I had been handed, fully expecting it to be some form of chimpanzee Identity Card, but inside the envelope there was merely a scrap of yellowing paper, on which was scrawled in a semi-literate hand,

'This man he get some chimpseys for sell!'

* * * * * * * *

CHAPTER 2
THE SUBURBAN CHIMPANZEE

So it was we arrived home at the Cape Estuary, not only with the usual assortment of local craftwork and curios, but also with an animated young chimpanzee and a wickerwork armchair Doug had the foresight to buy for him. It was only as we drove from the docks that uncertainty really set in at the enormity of being responsible for an entire ape. I had been told that Titan was two years old and he certainly seemed about the size of a child of that age, so I presumed that was how he would behave.

I wondered what my dog, Paddy's reaction would be towards the newcomer, but I need have had no fears on that score. Our steward had him bathed and looking unusually spruce and had kept him indoors to welcome us home. Mousa, who had come to supervise his friend's installation in his new home, strongly urged immediate introduction. Paddy was a dog of adventurous nature and diverse experiences, often staying away from home for days at a time, but from his astonished expression it did not appear that chimpanzees had previously been within his realms of acquaintanceship.

Titan, for his part, merely ignored Paddy and it was obvious he had encountered and mastered the handling of many a dog. He sat in the middle of the settee, like a guest, taking in the new surroundings. When Paddy dared lean forward to sniff a dangling foot, Titan shooed him away in no uncertain manner. Paddy contented himself in studying the hairy apparition from the other side of the room. It was instantly apparent who was to be boss!

I should have left it at that but Mousa picked Titan up and whispering in *Mandinka* into his oversized ear, lowered him towards the curious dog. Grudgingly, Titan extended the back of his hand towards Paddy's face and Paddy began licking the palm. This produced delighted chuckles from Titan who clambered down beside him, curling up in spasms of pulsating laughter. The more Paddy licked and nibbled, the more hysterical the grating laughter became, until Titan pushed the dog away and sat up breathlessly, cuffing tears from the corner of his eye.

I had even greater reservations at the prospect of introducing him to our steward. Landing was a middle-aged, scrawny man of a very serious disposition. There was something military in his bearing and his drawn sculptured face held the appearance of one who had just received unexpected, tragic news. Outdoors he always donned an antiquated faded bowler hat, which he brushed with loving attention each evening and would touch respectfully at passing those he considered worthy. It was a strange accessory to his flowing, embroidered *warrumba* which he wore on pray days. He regarded his domestic duties almost vocationally and clung stoically to Colonial protocol. He had been a batman to the British Army during the war and later held a responsible position at Government House. He had the effect of leaving me feeling somewhat unworthy of his exceptional services and totally incapable of living up to his expectations of me. When he had been recommended to us, we suggested he attend for the usual interview but Landing insisted he first look us over at a reception we were attending, where he was in charge of the bar. As we appeared to meet with his approval and measure up to his high standards, we were far too flattered not to accept. He tended more to interview us and Doug being a teetotaller counted greatly in our favour.

I fear our ways were sadly diverse, as I did not really want my home run with military precision. I would rather have liked to keep my saucepans in a cupboard of my choice, and slept on the right hand side of the bed but he persisted in sticking to the former memsahib's requirements and my nightie was always laid out on the left. The spare back bedroom continued to be referred to as 'Miss Deborah's room' in honour of some former young occupant. He declined to take an afternoon break as other peoples' retainers did, insisting he had too much work. He would still be dusting and polishing around me until supper time, looking worn and hot by the time he 'served dinner'. I felt a positive tyrant as he clanged pots and pans in the kitchen until late at night. We were not able to go to bed until he left as he insisted on turning down the beds and thoroughly 'pumping' the bedrooms. He would charge into the bedroom quarters with all the ferocity of a commando machine-gunning down the enemy, as he fired his overflowing *DDT* pump until it was empty and the contents dripped from the lamp-shades and saturated the floors. We would slip and slide our way into the bedroom, falling asleep with our eyes smarting and choking on the overpowering fumes.

Similar to his nightly assault on the mosquitoes, he concentrated his day-time attacks on germs by slopping around large quantities of a strong carbolic solution which would have taken the skin from my hands. Whilst doing this he would maintain a commentary of "killing de germs, must kill them all," pausing from time to time to take an appreciative sniff before continuing his assault. When the inspectors next visited us they queried why our expenditure on insecticides and disinfectant were so inordinately high and I can never catch a whiff of either product without recalling Landing vividly to mind.

Poor Landing, his presence so often saddened me, as he appeared an isolated relic from a superficial, pompous age. He was hardly, I considered, a likely person to become lackey to an ape. However, I had not allowed for the best British tradition, when our Colonial forebearers were indulged, if not encouraged, in their mild eccentricities which I now felt encumbent upon me to maintain.

Landing held himself in the highest esteem, regarding his peers as far inferior. When he told me he had waited on the Queen on the occasion of her visit, I naturally said how fortunate it had been for him, a rare honour. He was taken aback and appeared to imply that on the contrary, it was Her Majesty who had been fortunate to have been served by someone so practised in the art of table etiquette as himself. Not surprisingly, the phrase 'walk ten feet tall' originated in that part of the world and I doubt that 'inferiority complex' would translate into Mandinka.

As we drove in, Landing stepped out onto the veranda, wearing his best whites, giving the impression he had been hovering behind the curtains for some hours. He approached us with austere dignity, welcoming the master and mistress home. His glance took in Titan in a nonchalant way, if anything looking more askance at Mousa and instantly assessing him as a mere menial, directed him to the kitchen door. It was a constant source of embarrassment to me that Landing was unable to regard Gambian visitors as front-door guests.

"This is Titan" I said, as he did not seem inclined to comment on the hairy stranger in my arms.

"Yes Madam." He nodded, "I will fetch him some *chop.*" Would he like tea? He asked, as he held open the front door for me. It at least seemed Titan was to be regarded as a front door person, and he continued to act as if a chimpanzee was the one obvious occupant the house had formerly lacked.

I was now free to concentrate my misgivings on my other niggling doubts, which were Titan's state of domesticity and my lack of knowledge about chimpanzees. Half remembered stories, read and heard had begun to pervade my mind. Was it the Denises of 'Safari' fame, who had written about a chimp they were minding that had all but devastated their house? I did not think Doug would take kindly to that, as I glanced nervously around at his treasured possessions. Then there was one that had so fretted for his owner that he had died when left at a zoo. That must never happen to Titan, I resolved. Of course, one London chimpanzee had become an artist of some repute, maybe Titan could take up painting? I tried to concentrate on Gerald Durrell's Cholmondley who rode pillion on a motor-cycle, smoked a pipe and dropped in at the pub for a drink. He had made it sound so normal and such good fun, I began to wonder whether he did not somewhat play things down?

"Have you read any Gerald Durrell?" I hopefully asked Doug.

"No. He writes about the Greek Islands, doesn't he?"

"Yes, but he also had this marvellous chimp, Cholmondley, you really must read about him."

The ex-pat Britons I met did nothing to ease my apprehension, on hearing the news, Old West Coasters, who had lived most of their lives in Nigeria and Ghana, all seemed to end up in The Gambia, as if it were the end of the West Coast Road. They had seen it all before and nothing now surprised them. They nodded their heads sagely.

"You'll live to regret it." They unanimously warned relating the most hair-raising stories of previous animal-cranks who had taken on a chimpanzee. I tried to dismiss them as exaggerated West Coast gossip, as stories did tend to become embroidered in the re-telling over the years at 'The Club'.

The neighbours' reactions were not too encouraging, to say the least. They stood back as if eyeing me in reassessment, not realising they had harboured a lunatic in their midst! They expressed grave misgivings for the safety of their pets, as I tried to reassure them that chimps were not carnivorous, at least I did not think so.

I looked at Titan to reassure myself, a quasi-human-being, as he sat demurely in the wicker-chair we had bought him, whilst Landing waited upon him with endless cups of tea and digestive biscuits. His faithful dog, sitting adoringly at his feet, still hopeful of some tit-bit falling his way. A more angelical pair one could not wish to see!

I had always considered chimpanzees the most fascinating, adorable creatures apart from being amusing, imitative clowns and our closest relatives. I fully thought everyone must hold them in similar high regard. I wondered why this was not so?

My musing snapped off abruptly, as I realised Titan was no longer sitting in his chair and I noticed the mosquito screen had been removed from the open window, "He couldn't, he can't have. Why I can never budge that myself!"

But he had! His first escape did not prove too disastrous, he only wanted to explore his domain. I noticed our unfortunate neighbours who shared the compound, hastily dismantling the outdoor tea-table and retreating behind closed doors. They need have had no fear of his intruding, as tea-parties were secondary to the intriguing activities going on in our garden.

Landing had at once surmised that his new young charge would require some form of sleeping quarters and had accordingly summoned a suitable carpenter. Undaunted by the assignment, the man appeared to know exactly what was required, having built several cages for an animal collector, once based in The Gambia. He was in the process of sketching out a plan, tracing it with a screwdriver on the sandy soil of the lawn. Titan, arm around the carpenter's shoulder studied it with thoughtful approval, or so it seemed.

He could not have been more in his element, supervising the entire operation, he had no intention of coming indoors. He fetched and carried, knocked in the odd nail when a hammer was available and hovered around the boss-man, anxious and willing to please. I never again saw anyone who commanded quite that degree of respect from him.

"Dis not just be a cage, my *piccan ndemo*, dis be your happy home." The carpenter kept repeating, as Titan stared intently at his face.

I began to relax again, leaving him out there working, it seemed things might work out after all. There were obviously destructive chimps but Titan was more the constructive kind. Why just think of all those little jobs around the house I could find for him to do.

Long after dusk had descended, the workmen finished and Mousa had gone home, Titan was still out in the garden, refusing to enter his "happy home".

He sat up in the Flame Tree at the bottom of the garden, knocking nails into the branches and had obviously stolen the carpenter's hammer. I tried pleading, I tried shouting and had offered all kinds of food but replete from the high tea Landing had so lavishly served him, there was simply no tempting him down. I squatted lethargically beneath its wide canopy, the first of many trees under which I was to wait for Titan to choose to descend. The first twinges of up-river belly began to grip me or it could well have been some new down-river bug and by the time Landing discovered us, I had nodded right off to sleep.

He had returned from market laden with tropical delicacies which he felt his new charge would require. Without speaking, he jerked his head upwards indicating Titan's whereabouts and I wearily nodded my head.

Frugal with words, Landing would instigate a conversation with head inclinations or mime, which at times turned into a bizarre game of Charades, as I hazarded guesses. He would appear in the doorway holding up some item of food.

"Do we need some more?" "Is it bad?" "Are we having that for supper?" More infuriating was his predilection to the noun, "What's its name?", "What about the whats-its-name?", "Is the whats-its-name coming today?" "Plumber?", "Lobster man?"

Should I be entertaining, it would not deter him and visitors would find themselves joining in this parlour-like guessing game.

Titan, arm around the shoulder of the carpenter, studied it with thoughtful approval

"Hey, hey – hoop!" he boomed, quite startling me. He sounded just like a lion-tamer. "Titan – Come." He ordered.

Dropping his hammer, which narrowly missed my head, Titan scampered down instantly and clambered into Landing's arms. He consented to being placed in his new cage, after giving us both a goodnight kiss.

"Ha hum!" Landing coughed smugly, indicating it was merely a matter of the right approach. "See, Titan go to bed fine."

I gazed at my infallible retainer with a newly found respect!

We naturally hovered all evening, peering out into the darkness from time to time, as there still appeared to be sounds of movement from within Titan's hut. He seemed to be carrying out some form of inspection, testing the padlock which Landing had had the foresight to purchase, banging and tapping the woodwork and rattling the wire.

"Probably making sure he is burglar-proof!" I joked.

As Landing cleared away the supper dishes I could hear him repeating to himself

"Dis Titan, ha, he be too much fine." Leaving me in no doubt that he approved of him. I had at first found his habit of talking to himself quite disconcerting and had fully thought there was somebody out in the kitchen with him but at least it was never difficult to assess what was on his mind.

As dawn broke over the hitherto tranquillity of the residential Cape, where nothing more discordant than a cockerel crowing had formerly welcomed the dawn, a piercing, maniacal scream rent the air, ejecting everyone within a half-mile radius into a startled state of consciousness. This was followed by blood-curdling howls and some penetrating thuds. Doug and I jumped up and rushed out into the garden, as I was convinced that nothing less than a leopard must be savaging my little ape, locked helplessly in his cage. We were just in time to see the corrugated roof of his quarters do a vertical take-off, rapidly followed by Titan. His hair bristling, chest expanded, he emitted a few Tarzan-like calls, but rather than reminding me of Johnny Weissmuller, King Kong sprang to mind!

Tattoeing a few final thumps of bravado upon his inflated chest, he leapt down and was off and away. I took up a starting position and sprang athletically in pursuit with a speed I had not known I possessed, whilst my up-country/down country tummy gave a most painful lurch. I tried to fathom what change had befallen Titan as I sprinted along the road, for he bore so little resemblance to the tiny, demure chimpanzee who had captured my heart. He somehow seemed to have doubled in size overnight.

I was relieved to see him vault over the gate of the Agricultural Department Compound only a short way from our house as I doubted I could have maintained my pace much further. He was ensconced in a flourishing experimental grapefruit tree near the boundary but the gate was locked. I called to the night watchman whose legs I could see protruding from beneath an up-turned wheelbarrow where he had apparently sheltered from the damp night air. I was constantly amazed at African ingenuity in improvising with whatever was to hand, particularly in their total commitment to comfort. I had quite a fright the first time I entered the British High Commission building at night, when just inside the door I tripped over a recumbent form swathed in a Union Jack. It was not until the red, white and blue began wavering that I was assured it was alive and not some regimental corpse. The night watchman utilising it as a blanket.

"Cooey. Oow-oow! I say, Mr Watchman, can I come and get my chimp please?" I tried in vain to rouse the sleeping man.

When Landing pulled up breathlessly on his bicycle, solemnly raising his bowler, he appeared surprised to see me up and about so early, pirouetting on the corner, clad only in my nightie. "Hey, hey – hoop!" Landing bellowed the magic cry, leaving me wondering why I had not thought of it. Titan responded, vaulting over the gate towards Landing and climbed up onto the crossbar of his bike. Landing pedalled off along the road, chatting to Titan, and Titan amused himself dinging the bicycle bell.

How well they seemed to have taken to each other I thought, as I removed a small stone which had been embedded in the sole of my bare foot. It was certainly a pity about our close proximity to the Agricultural Department with its fruity experiments, it might as well be the Garden of Eden as far as Titan was concerned. I had wondered if we did not overfeed him, he might be more readily retrievable with the promise of food, but with such a lavish source on our doorstep, I fancied he could survive out for days. Until then I had viewed it as something of an asset as some of the less scrupulous employees sold rather delectable, locally unobtainable fruit.

By the time I arrived at the breakfast table, Titan was seated at the head of it, a serviette tied around his small neck. He was just lifting a spoon with a glace cherry on it up to his lips. Landing had segmented his grapefruit and sprinkled brown sugar on top and my favourite mug filled with tea was close to his hand. Doug was still sitting waiting and asked if I could find out what had happened to his grilled bacon, as he would have to leave for the office soon.

"Did Titan come and say good morning to you?"

"Dode Dow! He rad up and made a fuddy doise."

"Oh dear!" I cried, realising he was again nasal. "You haven't gone and caught a cold. I thought this warm, sea air would be good for your sinuses."

"Be careful!" I screamed as he got up and passed close to Titan. "Don't go too near him! I can't have him catching your germs."

I could not quite catch his parting comment, strange for it sounded just as if he had said "Don't worry, I won't."

He had no sooner shut the door when Landing appeared with the rest of the breakfast, a lightly-boiled egg for Titan with dainty, buttered bread fingers. Titan waited decorously as Landing took his empty fruit bowl from the left side and served his egg from the right.

"Where's Master?" Landing demanded, producing a plate piled high with bacon.

"He had to leave, Landing." I started, about to remonstrate on serving Doug's breakfast before Titan's, but on noticing his thunderous scowl as he slammed the plate down before me, I thought better of it. I definitely did not feel up to playing the Memsahib today.

"I'm sorry" I said instead, feebly. "He was late for the office. I'm afraid I really couldn't eat that bacon, my belly *palaver* me too much. I am sorry." I again apologised as the nauseating fumes of six greasy rashers assailed my queasy tum. "Could I just have a piece of dry toast please?"

Landing stalked back to the kitchen, leaving the offending bacon under my nose. He started muttering when once out in the kitchen,

"Oh no, master no *chop* bacon. Dee master already left. Eh. Em! Master he left. He go to the office." And so it went on.

My spirits lifted as I looked at Titan, dipping his soldiers in his egg and I was not sure whether I imagined it, but he seemed to give me an understanding smile.

"Toast!" Landing appeared at my elbow, banging down a barely tinged slice of bread. "Elbows off the table" he ordered and I instinctively put my hands in my lap, before realising it was Titan he was speaking to.

At least he removed that vile, imported bacon, it always smelt strongly of fish. A newly formed body of white lady vigilantes, who had even asked me to join, with consumer interests at heart had complained bitterly about the fishy bacon that arrived on these shores. They suggested it had been stored with the frozen herrings in the refrigerated hold of the ship. They were advised the tang was due solely to British pigs now being fed fish. Strange how everything at home seems to change when one's away!

I wondered how I could go about explaining to Landing that he should only cook one fishy rasher at a time, what tactic could I employ? The problem was that when the supply-ship called at Banjul, it was every memsahib for herself. A matter of stocking to the brim both fridges, all denying we managed to get anything, of course. It could well be months before we again saw bacon, but Landing deemed the object to be to dispose of it as fast as we could. Still, he was proved right last time, how smug he had appeared, when the ship's arrival was followed by a three day power cut and everything thawed and oozed in the fridge. I thought we would never get through the many pairs of strawberry ice-cream flavoured kippers!

Titan had polished off his breakfast, untied his serviette and smacked his chops. Landing appeared with flannel and towel to wipe his eggy face and hands.

"Mr Sey is waiting in the kitchen," Landing announced.

"Oh, the carpenter, come in Mr Sey" I called. "Would you like some coffee, Landing could you please fetch a cup."

"Yes please Mrs Morrison"

"He's had some in the kitchen." But Landing did reluctantly produce a battered, old tin mug.

"Now this is the problem." I started to explain to him how we were up against a creature with the power of ten of his best men. I still did not feel I had entirely convinced him of Titan's strength and wile, but a further two hours of attending to the reinforcement of his cage, were enjoyably passed by Titan. As he listened and assisted, fully occupied with the men, I was only too well aware that his interest was in the weaknesses of the construction and not the adulation of a fellow-artisan.

He appeared rather crestfallen when the workmen all departed, I expect he thought they were always there. If only they had have been, the problems I should have been spared! So as to occupy him, I took him and Paddy our dog down to the beach.

As I was setting out of the gate, Landing came after me brandishing two blue objects, which I realised were a child's bucket and spade.

"Where did you get those?" I asked

"The Wilson's steward, dee missus and *piccan* go away."

I took them, never entirely sure of the honesty of such indiscriminate borrowing that went on among the servants, unknown to their employers. There appeared to be some sort of taciturn acknowledgement of this custom among West-coasters and I had soon learned not to comment, when sitting down to a hostess's ornately laid table, "Oh, I have one of those." For the chances were, it was mine!

Titan clung to me as I carried him down to the beach, shrinking to his original diminutive size, nestling his head under my chin. The nearer to the sound of the ocean we got, the smaller he appeared to cringe. I set about making some sandcastles and mud pies, but he merely clung tenaciously on my back, not the least interested. I sat down and endeavoured to disentangle him, it was then that I discovered that there is no way of relinquishing a determinedly attached chimpanzee. Having the advantage of being quadromanous, no sooner has one disentangled a gripping hand, then an equally manipulative foot takes a firmer hold and it was rather like struggling with a four handed octopus. Paddy was most disappointed, as he ran in and out of the sea, hopeful that his new playmate would join him in his type of beach activities.

I trudged back home with him still nestling helplessly in my arms, his lips sucked in to appear the most defenceless, misunderstood creature that ever swung through a tree.

I had no sooner walked through the door with him, when he recoiled out of my arms and walking upright, appeared again to instantly double in size. He began chasing Paddy around the room wildly, waving the waste paper basket above his head, for added momentum. Paddy was quite overwhelmed, not having fully taken measure of his new friend and even I began to wonder if he really was trustworthy with domestic pets. I attempted a couple of rugby tackles, but he was too fast for me until I managed to ease open the french door for Paddy to make his escape. Titan was nearly out after him, when I grabbed a leg to pull him back.

"No. no, you naughty boy, you must not get out again." I chided. The ear-splitting scream that erupted took me completely by surprise, his face contorted, baring teeth and gums, Titan stamped and thumped the floor with his hands and finally, began throwing himself around the room violently, banging his head on furniture and walls. At the same time, he maintained one prolonged deafening wail of changing and louder pitch, without pausing for breath.

The more I ran after him and endeavoured to console, the more histrionic he became. Was he in some pain? I wondered. Could he be having a fit? I just hoped that I had not crushed his hand in the door and hurt those delicate fingers.

Landing, the gardener and Fatou, our washerwoman all ran in, all three shouting enquiries and adding to the melee. Neighbours' servants appeared on front and back verandas, together with several passers-by. Spontaneous rumour had it that the monkey had killed the dog, it seemed.

"What you do to him?" Landing shouted accusingly. "Hey hey Hoop!" but however loud he yelled his lion-tamer's call, Titan remained a volatile, heedless lunatic.

"Pick him up!" someone was shouting. As if it were possible to take hold of the writhing body. "Beat him!" cried another. I dreaded to consider the results of physical punishment when this performance had been precipitated by a mere verbal admonition. This maniacal, raging, wild beast was beyond my powers of conception - far removed from the cute, well-behaved chimps I had witnessed at Regent's Park tea-parties. I speculated as to how such discipline might be achieved; how little I knew!

We became so involved, shouting our discussion on strategy, that we failed to notice that the screeching had suddenly stopped. Titan sat cherub-like at our feet, sucking a thumb and looking up from one to another, as if endeavouring to ascertain what our problem might be.

"Ah, lookum, the *ndemo.*" Everyone began to croon and Landing picked up the demure chimp, for everyone to admire.

When I had first heard the word for chimp in *Mandinka* was '*ndemo*', it had at once struck me that it was an anagram of 'demon' and I had taken on a Titanic member of the species. How little, I then knew of the volatile nature of chimpanzees, particularly Titan's. He had a more pronounced personality than any chimp I have since come to know. When happy, none could be more uproarious, when thwarted, more obstreperous, when docile, more angelical and when loving, more affectionate.

I am never able to see a toddler having a tantrum without remembering Titan and by comparison the performance of the most raging child, seems no more than a mild fit of pique.

The ritual of getting Titan into his sleeping quarters at night, became increasingly arduous. Even the indominatable Landing was losing ground, and each ruse and tactic could only be used the once. We would each try in turn, the other two waiting behind the curtain, fingers crossed, bated-breathed, only to see Titan come bounding back in, triumphant. He seemed to consider the process great sport and the more frustrated we became, the funnier he seemed to consider it, rolling on his back pulsating with laughter.

The haul of food he would procure on a lightning raid on the kitchen, would be all that he was capable of carrying, obviously having first made a thorough recognoitre, waiting his chance. I soon learned that if the door of the room I was in slowly opened a fraction, followed by a pink, black-fringed face peering round at me, this was not the friendly prank I had at first thought – it was Titan, ascertaining if the coast was clear, before setting about some mischief. He would stagger from the kitchen with fruit, vegetables and cakes, not only in both hands, tucked under his chin, arms and in his groin, but also capable of carrying quite a large orange or potato in a foot. He would shuffle in, carrying his cumbersome load and having deposited his spoils on his chair, settled down for a feast. Should we try to retrieve anything or attempt to make him relinquish it, it would precipitate one of his fearful tantrums.

"We hear him laughing." My next door neighbour told me when she came in. "He seems very well behaved." She remarked, politely, her visit having coincided with his return from one of his prolific raids on the kitchen. Titan was munching his way through a few pounds of fruit and veg, neatly piling skin, pips and bruised fruit in a neat heap on the arm of his chair. I was so pleased at the good impression he was giving and one could not fail to notice the finesse with which he ate.

"I wondered if you had seen the plumber, he was supposed to have come yesterday, our bath is leaking and the floor swamped." She told me.

"Oh dear!" I laughed. "That explains it. When I came back from a walk yesterday morning our bath was in the middle of the front lawn and Landing told me the plumber had called." Our houses being identical with no distinguishing names or numbers, was a frequent source of confusion.

Having demolished his substantial snack, Titan came over towards us, adopting an air of levity and having taken a tissue from my pocket to wipe his hands and mouth, assessed the visitor to be a jovial sort and slapped her soundly on the knees.

"That's enough Titan." I said casually, trying to conceal my mounting apprehension, but he continued slapping her, with a smile of *bonhomie* spreading across his face. As he took the lady's hands and yanked her to her feet, I realised there would be no stopping him. With gay spontaneity he dragged her around the room, breaking into a square dance, he galloped with her around the dining table, a few breathless twirls in the kitchen, before dashing back into the lounge.

"Just leave go of his hands." I shouted, as I ran along behind.

"I can't." She cried, beginning to look quite giddy, as they maypoled around the settee at a furious pace.

Landing ran into the room 'hey-hooping' adding to the tumult but it only seemed to spur Titan on with greater zeal.

As they returned from a light fantastic down the hallway, Titan changed tempo to a more sedate gavotte, which gave me an opportunity to cut in. For a moment he looked as if he might be going to scream, but galloping him down the hallway I persuaded him it was a 'ladies' excuse-me.'

"I'll get on to the plumber." I called over my shoulder breathlessly as she made her escape. The poor woman looked quite exhausted and dishevelled as she stood outside taking a few deep breaths.

"Where dee madam go?" Landing asked, appearing with a tray of tea.

"Titan *humbug* her, so she left." I called, as my debonair partner twirled me around the room.

"Titan want to make dance." He complained peeved, at her unsocialbility when Titan had gone to such lengths to entertain our guest.

The tea was not wasted, both Titan and I were in need of it when he at last had had enough of dancing.

It was weeks before the plumber returned to re-install the bath, which afterwards sprang a persistent leak, bringing up the floor tiles. When the men came to re-lay the tiles, they dropped their tin of black gunge and left footprints all over the house. Three years later the bath was still leaking and the black splodges not entirely removed. I had discovered long ago in Africa it was better to grin and bear any minor inconvenience, rather than suffer the consequences of repair. The old West Coasters took the initials of the *Wolof* word 'wawa', which means 'yes', to represent 'West Africa Wins Again.' This was by far the most philosophical attitude to adopt and spared much frustration. People that struggled to maintain previous standards, whilst not quite succumbing to apoplexy, were prone to develop a nervous rash! The most quoted phrase in the Gambian vocabulary, which I had at first puzzled over was 'the next tomorrow'. This meant procrastinating until the day after tomorrow, which of course took even longer never to come than 'mañana.' A habit I readily adjusted to in the sticky climate.

Titan's reaction to Doug remained demonstrative but whether it was with affection I began to doubt. He would spring to his feet and emit a succession of prolonged hoots when Doug returned home.

"It's just his little chimpanzee way of greeting you." I would assure him. "You must remind him of his first owner." I was finding it increasingly difficult to visualise the patrician Frenchman who looked like Doug, but the reasons he had deemed it time to part company with Titan were becoming quite apparent.

Titan found our house a constant source of domestic complexities to be solved. It only took a few days to discover the fridge was opened by a foot pedal and he was quite capable of carrying a chair to stand on to reach wall cupboards, until there was nowhere to hide things from his reach. Landing began to carry the tin-opener around in his pocket, as opening a tin of evaporated milk was not beyond Titan's scope. He would still take tins when an opportunity presented itself, hiding them in his box and I would come across him trying to bang some object, like a toothbrush or spoon onto the top, trying to make a hole.

The three toilets which I had regarded as a luxury became a definite liability, as Titan ran from one to the other, delighting in flushing objects down. Catching hold of the ends of the toilet roll and twirling, he would make an entrance as a pastel-swathed mummy and I had to purchase them at least by the gross. He fortunately loved bathing and some peaceful moments could be obtained whilst he lathered and waded, letting out the water and turning on the taps to fill it up again. Having watched Fatou, he also enjoyed laundering, and on seeing him sneak out of the bedroom dragging a quilt, I would rush for my writing pad, knowing that fifteen minutes of harmless preoccupation were about to be enjoyed. Even though the bedclothes and towels he washed were already perfectly clean, it was well worth the sacrifice of a packet of soap powder.

Locks and keys were no puzzle to Titan and I suspect he had solved them at a far earlier age. In view of his fascination with anything mechanical, radios, cassette players, cameras etc had to be locked away, not to mention his dipsomaniac leanings. I once found him trying to pick the lock of the drinks cupboard with a hairpin.

This usually resulted in my never knowing where I had hidden a certain key, but left unattended, Titan would locate it instantly and always knew to which lock it belonged. In an unobserved minute he acquired the transistor radio, which had no batteries at the time. I watched as he twiddled and pressed all the buttons and thoughtfully scratched his chin. He jumped up on the sideboard and brought down the wire from the aerial, started poking that in the back. He was about to take the back off, when I thought it wise to cough and make my presence known.

However vigilant we were, he would always make at least one escape a day. During rare moments when I found him pensive and lost in thought, it was not difficult to imagine he was wondering how to get into the drinks cupboard or planning his next break-out. He never went far, usually a neighbouring garden but it would sometimes take hours to get him back. Before long I gave up trying to coax him down from a tree, I would merely take up position, squatting beneath it and came to know many people this way, although I would not go so far as to say I made friends! At first they were surprised to drive in or look from their window to find someone sitting underneath one of their trees, but gradually dismissed me as that strange woman and her monkey that often drop in.

Titan discovered a particularly prolific mango tree in a nearby compound and often aimed for it when he deemed the fruit would be ripe. Somehow, he always managed to evade the diligent gardener, Bakary, who was caretaking the empty premises, leaving me to explain what I was doing trespassing.

One afternoon when Titan was scrumping and I sat beneath the mango tree, Bakary was round the front watering when Titan chose to play a prank. Nipping down from the tree in which he was feasting he disconnected the hose from the tap. I scolded him and tried to catch him, but he ran back up into the dense foliage of the tree. By the time Bakary came on the scene, he discovered me trying to re-connect the hose.

"Why you spoil my water?" he asked in the manner of one resigned to such harassment.

"It wasn't me, it was my *ndemo*." I explained.

"*Ndemo*?" he said in disbelief. "I see no *ndemo*."

"Why you spoil my water?"

I pointed up to Titan, but he remained well hidden in the tree. Bakary re-connected the hose and proceeded to get on with his watering, casting suspicious glances back towards me.

No sooner was he out of sight, than Titan repeated the procedure. This time I was able to convince Bakary of Titan's presence, but when he glanced up at the hirsute angel, sitting aloft sucking on a mango stone, with the air of one incapable of the slightest misdemeanour, continued to suspect me. I heard him complaining to a passing fisherman.

"Dis *tubabo* (European), she go spoil my water. She say dee *ndemo* make *humbug*, but he na so."

I was to have further equally confusing encounters with gardener Bakary over the years.

I should not have been that surprised, when I discovered that the maxim 'Softly, Softly, Go Catch ee Monkey' originated in that part of the world, but however softly I pursued mine, I could rarely catch him!

I did befriend one delightful family through Titan who have remained great friends and I might otherwise have remained on merely nodding terms.

It was the afternoon Titan decided to sit it out in their *Gmlina* tree, stopping off on his return from the Agricultural Department where he had just lunched in sumptuous style.

On waking from siesta Marian Foon heard a voice outside the bedroom window whining plaintiffly, "Please, Titan, please come down, I want to go home." She looked out and called to her husband,

"Eh Kebba, there's a chimp in our *Gmlina* tree, won't the girls be pleased."

Never had Titan and I received such a welcome with typical Lancastrian hospitality. It was as if Marion had lived the twenty-odd years in her adopted country, merely in the hope that one day a chimpanzee might drop in.

"Does he take sugar?" She asked, as the whole family set about producing chairs and table under the tree in which Titan sat. Glancing at me, she intuitively surmised,

"Eh, you look as though you could do with a cuppa yourself."

Their two daughters, Baba and Candy, who had never before seen a chimpanzee, could not have been more thrilled at their tea-party guest. They thereafter became daily visitors and to this day, remain surrogate family.

The gesture was not wasted on Titan, he sat on the chair indicated to him and waited to be asked before helping himself to tea and biscuits. As he picked up his tea cup, he was a credit to me, even to the ultimate refinement of his little finger being crooked. When Marion assured him the tea-pot was empty, after his third or so cup, he impolitely left the table and returned to his tree.

"Oh no!" I cried in desperation. "Now I'll never get him down."

"Don't worry, I'll think of something" Marion assured me sympathetically, assessing hysteria was about to set in.

With her natural alacrity, she instructed the crowd that had gathered to watch the chimp's tea party outside their gate to follow us all down the road.

"You see," she explained "Where I think you have been going wrong, is in following him, instead of letting him follow you." So we all marched purposefully out of their compound, leaving the stubborn chimp alone up in his tree.

"Come and join us." Marion urged the stragglers with all the zeal of a Salvation Army campaigner, as we marched down the road with our substantial band falling in regimentally behind, puzzled at the object of the exercise.

On finding himself abandoned, Titan soon came scuffling at the rear, glancing back over his shoulder, trying to assess what danger we were all retreating from.

Some visitors, who had just arrived at our house, were somewhat perplexed at the approaching procession, as out of the corner of my mouth I beckoned them to follow us in. For a while, it had seemed that all our followers were also going to march in behind us, assessing the object to be a spontaneous party, but Landing soon rushed out to banish them, shouting in sergeant-major-like tones,

"Hey, Her, Ha! Attah!" (clear off!)

I fear we lived somewhat public lives at the Cape, as our house was en route from village to beach, which the majority of

As we marched down the road with a substantial band falling in behind.

Bakau inhabitants sauntered along in the course of the day. The gate was adjacent to the raised goldfish bowl living room and it was rather like living permanently on a stage, always assured of a packed and appreciative audience. Prior to having Titan we had felt somewhat inadequate, doing little more entertaining than sitting reading. Each time I looked up there would be somebody waving until it became a reflex action to keep raising my arm, automatically in the manner of royalty. We often suspected that the residents of Bakau, when finding they had nothing better to do, would suggest a stroll to the beach and see what the Morrisons were up to. With Titan now in residence, gala entertainment was guaranteed! Even so the crowds were not quite as multitudinous as when we had first moved in. We had puzzled at the numbers that gathered to stand and gape in awe and hardly anyone ever came in. After a couple of weeks, a young lad apparently elected to act as spokesman, ventured cautiously up to the door.

"Please sir, when are you going to fire it?" He asked Doug who was a baffled as I.

"Fire what?" we asked

"D.d.d.dat – c.c.c.canon." He pointed to Doug's telescope.

We explained what it was and let him look through it and enlightened he called to tell his friends. They relaxed and as word obviously went around the village, we were viewed with less suspicion.

I had wondered why Landing had stood on display always cleaning it, playing to the crowd at the gate, in rather the manner he demonstrated the vacuum cleaner, or "my machine" as he referred to it as most people used brooms. Doug had left the telescope in the screened window, where it would get the maximum breeze to protect the lens from humidity, without thought for need of explanation.

Titan struck up a lively friendship with Baba Foon, my neighbour Marion's youngest, who had the energy to join his more rumbustious games. Alas it came to a sudden and painful conclusion, when one Sunday he took a bite at her hand. We rushed her off to the hospital, being familiar with Sunday afternoon casualty procedure when Doug had been bitten by a dog a few weeks before. We left a young Gambian friend of Titan's in the house in charge of him, but on our return, neither of them were to be found.

It accounted for the crowd I had seen gathered down near the beach as we drove in. Sure enough, I found Titan clinging half way up a prickly palm tree, his face spread in a wide grin of terror, as the throng taunted and teased. I had no problem in retrieving him, as he screamed out to me, so relieved to see me, and clambered into my arms. Young Abdoulie explained that when he tried to stop Titan opening the bureau just after we left, he had flown into one of his tantrums and the poor lad had panicked and ran out leaving the door open.

Baba and her parents regarded the injury as nothing other than a normal incident in her life, as she did tend to be prone to the more unusual injuries. As I saw for myself some time later, when she had two fingers speared together by a fish's fin.

Those first few weeks with Titan were one insane, chaotic state of confusion. Although Landing did his best, encouraging his rapidly improving table manners, allowing him to smoke and dressing him in his son's cast off school uniform, which was not at all the type of development I had had in mind for him, and I hoped had rescued him from.

His talents that impressed me were more of a natural kind. His ability to self-forage, albeit in some neighbour's garden and his demonstration of how to fish termites. Having selected a suitable twig or blade of dried grass, he would poke this into an opening in a termite nest. Then when assessing he had sufficient, would flick it out and scoop off the writhing insects into a suitable wodge and eat them.

I realised the situation was getting desperate when I came out of the bath one day to find no sign of Titan, Landing or Fatou. They returned a few minutes later, puzzled that I should scream,

"Where did you take him."

"Why, down to the beach." Landing said. "Some Swedish tourists go bathing, they like Titan too much, look what they give him."

Landing was jingling some coins and Fatou smiling delightedly,

"We get 3s.6d." She proudly told me.

They were unable to understand why I should be anything other than pleased, as I reasoned he could have well bitten one of the tourists, and as many of them did not bother with clothes, my mind boggled at the expanse of tempting flesh revealed for him to take a bite.

When Titan first came to live with us I had so looked forward to our painting together. I had once seen some paintings which had been done by a chimp, and whilst not altogether appreciating the finer points of the abstract pictures, the critics had acclaimed them. I had fully taken it that all chimpanzees were artistically inclined.

I had visualised us sitting companionably at respective easels, both engrossed in our work, "Pass me the burnt umber, Titan?" I would ask him, for he would naturally have readily learned the names and values of the respective colours. Why, we might even have held a two-man exhibition!

Apart from the fascination of squeezing out the entire contents of a tube on palette and displaying a distinct preference to vermillion, which he would daub all over his face, he appeared quite devoid of talent.

Painting the house appealed more to his workmanlike nature, and when a man arrived to paint the outside walls, he was most anxious to assist. Wielding the large brushes and splashing paint everywhere, was more to his taste and although the man told me he had never had a better assistant, I did not feel it was quite the case.

* * * * * * * *

CHAPTER 3
THE BREWER MENAGERIE

In desperation, I rang the Forestry Officer about whom I had heard a great deal. Each time I mentioned wildlife, his name would crop up and Landing had frequently commented, when I despaired of doing anything with Titan.

"Mr Rhubarb" (which appeared to be his rather unusual name) "He *savvy* Titan too much" and I would hear him muttering to himself praising the man, as he worked around the house, "He be fine man."

I had met Mr and Mrs Rhubarb briefly at a reception when we had first arrived. I had already heard so much about the remarkable family and they were held in such high esteem, to almost be honorary Gambians. One only had to mention them from Banjul up to Fatoto and someone would beam with recognition saying:

"Rhubarb be fine man."

I had seen them apologising as they arrived late at the reception, saying they had been unavoidably detained due to having to feed an eagle and something about a *solodingo* (a small leopard) getting out.

From what I had heard at the Club, the fellow was something of a Dr Dolittle and lived with his family in a Game Park called *Abuko.* I was longing to visit it, they had founded it themselves apparently and they both looked the part. Although dressed for a formal occasion, I did not fail to notice a little mud on the hem of the lady's dress and her silver sandals were studded with teeth marks, of some young animal it seemed and one of the straps seemed to have been chewn off. A situation I was not unfamiliar with myself.

I was surprised to notice that Mr Rhubarb walked with a pronounced limp, as each time I had asked after him, I had been told he was 'on trek'. Somehow giving me the impression that he trampled the width and breadth of the country on foot. I discovered he did actually travel by Land Rover, 'on trek' being the equivalent of an East African 'safari'. His lumbering gait did nothing to detract from the image of 'Big Bwana Game' and I imagined it must have been the result of a hunting accident or he had been mauled by a big cat.

"This is Mr and Mrs Rhubarb" my Gambian companion introduced.

"How do you do? Are you liking The Gambia? We've been here many years." Mrs Rhubarb graciously smiled. "You and your husband must come out for *chop* one evening." She invited cordially.

"How do you do?" Mr Rhubarb slowly enunciated, his light blue eyes twinkling from beneath unruly silver eyebrows. His cheek-bones were creviced with fine lines, as though he were permanently squinting outdoors in the tropical glare.

"Make you shake my left hand, I hope you don't mind." It was only when he drew my attention to it, that I realised his right hand was swathed in a blood-stained hankie.

"Oh dear!" I said. "Has something attacked you?"

"No, just caught it in the car window, a silly thing to do. The glass keeps falling out."

He then proceeded to recount the most fascinating bush stories, as a crowd gathered around. He told us about the animal orphans they were rearing and how he had at last raised funds to fence off *Abuko* Reserve. It was now a matter of dissuading the poachers, when somebody asked if they were not deterred by the Ninkey Nanker and I asked what this was.

"Ninkey nanker one big bad spirit that lives in *Abuko,* some people say it looks like a giant snake and not many people dare venture in there at night."

"What sort of snake is it?" I asked interested, taking it to be some indigenous species of which I had not heard.

Mr Rhubarb went on elaborating, until I realised he was pulling my leg and the Ninkey Nanker was in fact a myth, that cropped up in most localities but it at least helped protect *Abuko.*

I was even more drawn towards the man's character when on pulling another blood-stained hankie from his pocket a cluster of unshelled peanuts fell out and the state of his dark trousers indicated that he had recently sat in some straw. The entire family appeared totally dedicated to the preservation of Gambian wildlife, to the exclusion of everything else and my admiration for them rapidly grew.

I must say, I was equally impressed with his animal impersonations, as one who had aspired to such mimicry herself. His hyena calls were so realistic, that an oriental diplomat who had been standing close by us, rapidly retreated into the house.

When I was at last able to get hold of him on the phone in connection with the problems I was having with Titan, he pointed out that the name was actually Brewer, which is difficult for Gambians to pronounce.

"A chimpanzee, eh! They can be tricky I believe, though I've never had one myself." He did not sound very encouraging. I enumerated the difficulties I was having and told him I would be grateful for any advice he might have.

The Brewers kindly agreed to have Titan whilst we had larger, stronger quarters constructed. Mr Brewer further explained that it would be a wonderful Christmas treat for his daughter Stella, who was arriving for the three week school holidays. She had grown up with a pet monkey, so caring for a chimp would be most appreciated.

I had barely heard the weekly plane fly in, when a truck carrying a large cage drove in. (It appeared more suitable for King Kong himself!) It was unloaded by the driver and a lovely looking blonde girl in safari attire. I have retained a snap-shot image of that first encounter, Stella was instantly transfixed by Titan and he with her. Stella's destiny seemed to have been sealed in that instant, for she was to go on to dedicate her life to become a forerunner in chimpanzee rehabilitation.

I did feel that she was a little disappointed in Titan's baby-like 'butter wouldn't melt' manner, from the gauntlets she wore and the cage, she appeared braced to wrestle with a savage beast. Instead of which, he snuggled in her arms, shrunken to infant size.

I felt quite lost without Titan. The house was unnaturally tidy until I found myself longing for a little of his brand of chaos.

Whilst staying with the Brewers, Titan began to shed his milk teeth, which indicated he was far older than the two years we had been lead to believe and he was more likely to be five or six. Titan now grinned appealingly through a front gap and I realised that he would soon near adolescence and his time with us would be limited. It was obviously the reason his former owner had deemed

Stella meets Titan

it time to part with him. Stella had kept one of his teeth to take back to her biology teacher, hoping that such a rare specimen might appease her into overlooking uncompleted homework. I could well imagine she would have had little time for homework with Titan around.

When we arrived at *Yundum* to visit the Brewers, we had some difficulty in finding their house. Some small boys eventually directed us and when they realised who we were, all proudly showed us their healing wounds, almost competitively. It seemed Titan had made his presence known in the locality and bitten most of the children who had wanted to play with him. One poor little chap was most chagrined as he had not been bitten at all and had no scars to take back to England when he returned to school.

I must admit to a sense of disillusion when we finally located their house, a modest Government dwelling drastically in need of repair in a crescent of identical houses. How on earth had they managed with Titan I wondered in horror, with Christmas guests staying as well. I had fully imagined this remarkable family in some rambling, old colonial house set in the heart of the reserve, with antelopes grazing on the lawn.

I knocked on the wooden screened door to the veranda and by the state of the mosquito netting, it appeared that was where the antelopes actually grazed, or something did. Having called out and knocked for some minutes, I ventured around the back. Doug wondered whether I had mistaken the evening and said he would prudently wait outside in the car. Outside the back door a white, spectral shape flatulated and I recoiled at the thought of the Ninky Nanker, until realising it was the white uniform of their cook performing his evening prayers.

"I say! Hello!" I called. "Are Mr and Mrs Brewer at home?"

He paused, mid-undulation, hands still suspended in the air, his plump face regarding me for some seconds before replying,

"Mr Brewer and Missie Stella and Hedder, day be up dee Reserve. Dee Madam she bathing. Wait small time in dee house."

We sat uncertainly in their living room and even I began to wonder if we had not arrived too early and Doug was still insisting we had come on the wrong night. I could see the dining room table, so I crept over to see how many places were laid. As I approached, something jumped off it, which I had first taken to be a rat. I realised it was a mongoose and from the state of the white tablecloth, it appeared to have been eating the accompanying garnishes from an hors-d'oeuvre tray.

"It's alright, there are six places." I staged whispered to Doug. "I think it might be curry, I can smell it, can you?"

"Do" he answered nasally. "I've still got this cold."

Just then Mrs Brewer came into the room.

"I am so sorry we weren't here to greet you. We've had a bush fire up at the Reserve. I do hope Eddie and the girls won't be too long. Now what can I get you to drink?"

I shot a meaningful glance at Doug, indicating that I was right and we had been expected after all.

Mr Brewer and his two daughters returned a little later, so blackened with soot, I barely recognised them when they came through the door.

"Oh sorry, I didn't know we have company." Eddie apologised as he came in.

Doug shot me a counter-glance!

It took me some time to get attuned to the family dialect and Doug did not seem to understand it at all. They had lived in The Gambia for so long that they instinctively conversed in a form of pidgin to each other, quite unconsciously I am sure. It must have been a boon to foreign speaking visitors, but British newcomers must have at first wondered whether they had stumbled across some remote, lost, white tribe.

"Make you go feed dem *piccans* now Hedda." Eddie said.

"Na Pa, make I get *chop* first. I go small time."

"Dere be small bit breeze. Small time big rains come."

The strange dialogue was accompanied with exaggerated gesticulating to each other, as if not quite sure how much English they each understood.

"Come!" Eddie beckoned, slowly raising his opened arms. "Make we all go *chop*."

After their cook, Abu, had served me with rice and curry, telling me, as he did so, about some old relative of his who had just died, Lilian passed me an empty dish.

"Have some small *chop*." She invited.

Not wanting to appear rude, I pretended to take something and passed it into Eddie's outstretched hand.

"Oh Ricky." He shouted, "He go t'ieve dee small *chop* again. Who *savvy* where he go?"

Stella and Heather, wearing scowling expressions, shielded their hands over their eyes, turned their heads in unison, as if looking around the room, Sailors' Hornpipe fashion. The two girls appeared to be very close to each other, almost like twins.

"Ah ha!" Stella cried. "Dare he be." As Ricky's face appeared from inside a silver ice-bucket, which was filled with monkey apples and some unfamiliar dry pods.

"Hey, get out of dare. Now he go t'ieve Dembo Bojang's *chop*."

"Which man be Dembo Bojang?" I asked, feeling I was getting into the swing of their speech. They all laughed uproariously and I took it to be due to the strange way I spoke.

"Na. Dembo Bojang na be man, ee be *piccan*, vervet monkey, get small bit sick arm. *Chop* some." Heather offered me one of the brown, curled pods. It had a pleasant flavour, almost a caramel tang, but did not go too well with the curry.

"Oh dear, you must excuse me." Lilian began yawning. "I na go sleep all night Bagh!" Her pidgin was slightly different to the rest of the family and I thought I detected a Welsh inflexion in her voice. It was possible to imagine that she had once lived in some lush green, Welsh-speaking valley, leading a perfectly conventional life. Whereas with the other three, it was not too wild a stretch of the imagination to believe that they had been born and reared in total isolation in some remote part of the bush.

"Timmy, he go keep biting my foot." Lilian complained.

Timmy Tim it transpired was their genet (small spotted cat) and an unfortunate creature to have in the bedroom at night, being nocturnal. Poor Lilian, she did appear to have a great deal to endure living in this haphazard menagerie. I winced when I speculated the havoc Titan had doubtlessly reaped.

"Olly, Olly, Oo." Eddie suddenly called, startling me.

"Olly olly oo. Olly Olly oo!" the two girls also took up the call, when Abu slowly appeared and proceeded to serve the dessert, going round the table paying no heed to the chanting. So I took it to be a family custom to indicate to the servants they were ready for pudding. Most West Coasters rang dainty china or brass bells to summon their servants but the Brewers did not appear to conform at all.

"Please Madam. My feet *humbug* me too much." Abu told Lilian, the complaint obviously triggered by her mentioning her own.

"Alright Abu, make we go see doctor next tomorrow."

I noticed as he went out that the fronts of his white drill shoes had been cut out and blanco was smudged over his toes. I wondered what was wrong with them, but felt he might well tell me. He appeared to be a very old and lethargic man.

"Olly olly oo. Olly Olly oo!" They began chanting again, just as I was about to tuck into my fruit salad. I put down my spoon in case they were calling for jelly or cream to go with it.

"Please Master, Olly done come." Abu shuffled in again, dangling a piece of raw meat on a toasting fork.

Now I really did not know whether to start my sweet or not, as it appeared we might be going to have some form of Gambian Fondue, flambéd at the table in lighted palm wine, no doubt.

Just then two large eyes appeared looking in the window, staring unblinkingly, looking as perplexed as I was beginning to feel. It was soon apparent that this was the Olly they had all been calling, an owl they had reared and released, but who still liked to drop in at supper-time for a bite to eat.

Eddie went over to him at the window and communicated in a succession of well-rounded quavering O's, which Olly responded to. He took the meat Eddie proffered and flew off hooting his farewells.

"Ee sometimes go hoot wid laughter." Eddie grinned.

I smiled and wondered whether it was now safe for me to start eating my delicious looking sweet.

We all went through to the lounge and Abu brought the coffee in, everyone sitting silent and replete.

"My wife she make no more *piccans*." Abu said to no-one in particular, as he served the coffee.

"Oh no!" I replied politely.

"When I be small I be a tall man." He continued, as we went round with the sugar and milk. "Den I get dis sick for dee liber." He added, his face coming close to mine as he offered the sugar.

"Oh dear, how nasty." I said.

"Make we go feed dee *piccans*." Heather said to Stella and each donning a gauntlet, they went out into the dark.

"Please Madam, you na see my big stick spoon?" Abu asked.

"No" I answered, thinking he was still speaking to me.

"I get it" Heather shouted in through the open window. "I take it to feed dis big bird. Abu, make ee gib me Charlie's stout."

I had the impression there was a strange snorting sound behind me and when I turned to look out of the window, I was aware of something looming behind Heather, large and white. Abu handed Heather a bottle of Guinness which she appeared to be giving to a scrawny horse. I stood up so that I might see it better and the pathetic creature certainly seemed to be enjoying his evening tipple.

"Make ee no get drunk." I quipped, adopting their patois. Heather really laughed, more heartily than my little jest warranted I felt, but she then explained.

"He go get drunk last yesterday when he chop all dee mangoes that get too much fit." "Dis soon make you a big fat boy Charlie." She assured the dipsomaniac steed.

"I want my stick spoon in dee kitchen" Abu was still saying, as he shuffled off on his obviously painful feet. At least he did not talk to himself in the kitchen, I speculated, as Landing did.

"Jan, come lookum." Stella was calling from the veranda, as she pulled in two young hyaenas on dog leashes.

"Day be fine big *piccans* now" she told me, as she patted them soundly on the rumps. "Here you feed one" she offered me a feeding bottle.

I had never been that close to hyaenas before and even at that tender age, their jaws looked massively powerful and they made the most persistant, demanding wails. I thought they appeared rather large to still be having a bottle, mine nearly yanked it out of my hand, but she told me they were only a few weeks old.

"Careful ee no go bite you, he make *humbug* sometimes." Stella warned, making me even more wary.

"Heather and I we be up all night to gib dem *chop* when dese *bukis* small. Now make you wipe his bottom."

"Pardon" I said

"Look, make you do it na so." She demonstrated, explaining that it stimulated defecation after they had eaten, as their mother would have normally licked their anus for them, otherwise they could develop some fatal colic. Only she did not put it in quite those words, still using the quaint family verbal shorthand.

"Tell him a joke Jan, see if you can make him laugh." Eddie called out.

"Oh, laughing hyaena, I see." I said, trying to laugh like one myself.

Then Eddie told us some of his shaggy wild animal stories but I felt some of them might not have been so shaggy. Feeling I knew them a little better, I asked him what was the matter with his leg.

"I go fall off the back of a lorry when I be a young man" he told me, but I was not too sure whether he was joking and did not like to laugh.

When I had to go to the bathroom, I pushed open the door cautiously, fully expecting to meet a ten foot python curled up around the loo, as such tales were rumoured. I was certainly surprised at what I did discover when I switched on the light. It at least accounted for the buzzing noise I had been aware of all evening, which suddenly droned deafeningly near. In the bath there was a huge piece of bee-hive, draining honey into a bucket.

"Go softly, mind dee bees." Somebody cautioned, but too late, I had already been stung. I could not help but speculate how they managed to bath.

"Make you wash your hands in dee kitchen" a voice called through the door.

"Honey gets sensitive to dee smell of soap." Eddie explained when I came out.

"My goodness! Who go chop dis new cushion?" Lilian was saying as I came back into the room. I cast a nervous sympathetic smile in her direction. I marvelled at the tenacity of the woman that she had not long ago given up trying to create a comfortable home in this overcrowded ark.

A large spotted feline with stripes on it's back came stalking into the room.

"Oh, what's that?" I asked, in awe.

"Dis be Charlie, *solodingo* a serval cat you know." So they had another Charlie, it was not surprising they ran out of new names.

I bent to stroke him and to my delight he jumped on my lap. His purring vibrated thrillingly, as he kneaded my lap with his claws. Then in came their old ginger tomcat, who also made straight for my lap and edging Charlie off, settled down himself. They told me that Ginger-puss was their boss-animal and the longest staying four-footed inhabitant of the house.

I looked across at Doug to see what he thought of the serval but his face was obscured by a long striped tail. It was Timmy Tim, the sleek, elongated spotted genet, who was curled up around Doug's neck like some exotic fur collar. These cats really are so exquisite, I thought.

"What have you done dear?" I asked as Timmy flicked his tail down. "Did you cut yourself shaving?" I had not previously noticed the sticking plaster on his chin, but he could not answer, for Timmy's tail brushed in his mouth as he opened it to speak.

"No, Timmy just scratch him, only small t'ing." Stella said.

It really had been such a pleasant evening, I had been so fascinated with all the animals that shared their house and was sorry when it was time to leave. It had not been at all stiff and starchy as most of the dinner parties we had attended, and they really were the most warm, unpretentious people one could wish to meet on African soil. Exactly how I had expected to find white Africans when I first went to Rhodesia, but Salisbury was barely different from Bromley, except the ladies shopped in long white gloves and sometimes even wore Ascot hats. No, the Brewers were definitely more my sort of people and no wonder Titan had so enjoyed staying with them.

I said I hoped they would come to visit us and Titan. They had certainly inspired me with a new confidence in my approach to my wayward ape.

"Did you enjoy it dear?" I asked Doug going home in the car, realising he had contributed very little to the conversation but he was a taciturn man at best. “Isn’t that serval gorgeous and my goodness those hyaena cubs?”

“I liked that radio Eddie’s got.” He said at last. “He told me he can pick up London quite well.”

* * * * * * * *

CHAPTER 4
SLOGGING OVER AFRICA

A large cage in the garden had been built while Titan was staying with his new friends and he appeared to approve of it. I had personally assisted and supervised the construction, only too well aware how doubly secure it had to be finished. However on his primary inspection of his new quarters, Titan at once found a weakness in the door. It was only a matter of pushing on the upper planks across the top, which he soon put his fist through and burst out triumphantly, only to be confounded by a second door. I was certainly glad we had been guided by Eddie and fixed double doors. A must for hairy escapees.

For some reason the carpenter had seen fit to put an inside bolt on the door, not a wasted amenity, as Titan would snap it shut whenever he was at home. He appeared to appreciate the privacy and independence it afforded him, although he could not always be persuaded to open it when I wanted to go in with him.

We had provided him with a grid window, with wide wire squares, through which he could receive his visitors and any gifts they may have brought him. A table and chair fitted adjacently, on which his frequent and sumptuous meals were served. His friends from the village were delighted to see him back in residence and continued to bring delicacies that we were not always able to obtain, avocados and out of season fruit.

"We haven't had a mango for ages." Baba would complain, as she watched Titan tuck into several.

Titan did not have to spend too much time in his quarters, as well furnished as they were with swinging ropes, tyres and perches and a cosy sleeping cage with a vast selection of educational toys. We now spent most of our days trampling around the bush with Landing and Paddy. We hacked a path through the overgrown scrubland that backed onto our house and forged a route to skirt the beach, through to the mangrove swamps. During Titan's absence, we had seen very little of Paddy but with such an invigorating daily jaunt in the offering, he now waited each morning outside Titan's cage. Landing or I had to carry Titan as we set out, as it was not the type of terrain he liked to cover on foot. He gazed around regally, like some Eastern potentate being conveyed by his devoted retinue, his stomach gurgling noisily from the large mugs of breakfast tea. Among the stunted, hacked at trees, which had long since been hewn for firewood, there was one large flourishing tree with overhanging branches. This had been preserved as it was used for annual initiation ceremonies, which took place under its shaded canopy. This was Titan's favourite stop, where he was able to demonstrate his acrobatic skills to the full. Scampering along and swinging from the branches, with Paddy barking encouragement below. Titan would leap down from lofty heights to pounce on his canine friend and give his tail a friendly tug, scurrying back up convulsing in throaty chuckles, as Paddy attempted to pursue and nip his vulnerable, hairless posterior.

They would chase each other endlessly around fallen trees and obstacles, suddenly changing direction, the pursuer becoming the pursued in their special version of 'it'. On the whole, they appeared pretty well matched, although I tended to caution Titan not to be too rough with Paddy, whilst Landing took the opposite view. An altercation breaking out between us, whilst the animals continued their romp, regardless.

We gradually weaned Titan onto the beach, starting in the mangrove shrubs, the weird saline miniature trees, formed an arena when the tide was out. Here Titan felt safe to play in the damp sand, as wild chimps would never venture out into the open, away from trees, where they would be vulnerable to attack by predators. He loved to chase the vast armies of crabs that patrolled the swamps, stamping his feet and slapping his hands on the ground, revelling in the power he commanded. Until Paddy would blunder in, unwittingly driving the crabs towards Titan, who would dash to me to pick him up.

Paddy was able to take advantage of Titan's natural fear of water by wading in up to his ears, hippo-fashion, and enjoy a respite from his indefatigable friend's endless pranks. It was difficult to assess the depths of the tidal pools, as they constantly changed and I had feared Titan might suddenly sink into a steep banked lake, intent on pursuit of Paddy. I underestimated his powers of reasoning, as I so often did, for he would approach any water most prudently, first finding a stick to place in the water to take a sounding, before placing so much as an opposable toe in it. If the stick went down at all far, Titan would leap back promptly.

We would make our way back, far more wearily than we had set out, stopping at Titan's favourite trees in late afternoon. Titan soon discovered several fruiting varieties that were not only edible but quite delicious and quenching at the end of a day's trek.

Whilst we non-arboreal creatures rested beneath the shade of a tree, Titan would build himself a nest above us, finding a suitable leafy fork. He would bend over stems of leaves and gather extra foliage when necessary, displaying innate behaviour and constantly teaching me about wild chimpanzees. I wondered whether it was instinctive or remembered skills and how old he had been when first snatched from his rightful domain.

It was a most bedraggled party that arrived home, Landing and I scratched and grubby, Paddy panting wearily at our heels, his sand encrusted coat, speckled with burs. Only Titan retained the same surging vitality he had set out with. He would at once get out his box of treasured possessions and study them like a miser counting his money.

If fortunate enough to have a screwdriver hidden away, he would then set about removing screws from door-hinges, electric points or dismantle some new-found component he had managed to get his hands on.

Towards dusk we would take Titan out to his quarters with the inducement of a large assortment of his favourite food, not least being a watered beer, which became his ritual night-cap. With supper devoured, he would climb up to the top of his cage and look around in all directions and coming over to bolt his door, would then settle in his sleeping quarters. Provided he was left in peace, he would settle down not stirring until morning. Should we remain outside his cage, to sip on a sundowner, he would swing over, flailing his arms and hoot his displeasure in no uncertain manner.

He would not tolerate neighbouring parties either and when one was in progress nearby, he would clamber in and out of his sleeping box, climbing up to glare in the offending direction and his protracted calls were not difficult to interpret as meaning:

"Belt up over there, there's a chap here trying to get some sleep."

He would be in the foulest of moods the following morning, had he not been allowed his full twelve peaceful hours.

The relationship between Titan and Doug had not improved, if anything it appeared worse. After his initial charging, hooting display when Doug came home, Titan would then sit uneasily occupied, quite distracted by his presence. I must admit, whilst Doug was there he was a paragon of domestic virtue, as I was always pointing out. I was at constant pains to list his good points, how no damage was ever sustained at Titan's hands, why he even used the best china and drank from glasses and had never broken a thing. I always hastened to re-screw any door-hinges or objects he had loosened and made a thorough check of such things before Doug's return. Titan would sit flicking through a book or brushing his hair, half-heartedly, glancing at Doug from time to time. Every so often compelled to swagger over to him, expanded to his full height, letting forth a series of argumentative grunts over the side of Doug's chair.

Like the plot of any true Western movie, the time came for confrontation, only rather than a shoot-out in a deserted street, it was more of a bite-out in a chimpanzee's cage.

It was a Sunday afternoon and Landing had been persuaded to take an unaccustomed day off and as we were going out, we were endeavouring to lure Titan into his quarters earlier than usual. Each time I had tried to walk into his cage with him, he had clung to the doorway, inextricably with hands and feet, his fearful screams shattering the Sunday, siesta silence. Doug eventually stated he would have no more nonsense and took Titan into the cage himself, taking him unawares. Once inside, Titan hurled himself at the closed door in a positive fury and performed his ritual tantrum. Doug pulled him away from the door so as to get out when Titan lunged at him, biting his hand, which instantly spurted blood. When Titan attempted a second charge, Doug came at him, cuffing him and shouting and generally letting him know he was the dominant primate in this territory.

Rather than fly into an even greater fury, as I had expected, Titan sat cowering and whimpering in the corner of his cage. I dreaded to contemplate the consequence on their future relationship.

So for the third time we interrupted the casualty doctor's Sunday cricket and he was beginning to view us rather dubiously. The man must have wondered what bizarre activities took place at the Cape on Sunday afternoons.

Doug went out that evening with a conspicuously bandaged thumb, only to meet Eddie Brewer with a similarly bandaged finger. They were able to compare bites and swap animal stories, vying as to who had suffered the worse injury. The subject seemed to be coming an habitual topic of discourse at such gatherings, throwing Doug into the unaccustomed limelight. Although I suppose it was rather a drastic route to social acclaim!

I viewed Doug's arrival home from the office the following evening with some trepidation. Titan appeared uneasy and had jumped up to look out of the window several times, as the appointed hour neared. At first sound of the car, he was on his feet and stamping and leaping by the window and in a fervour of excitement by the time Doug emerged from the garage.

"Don't come in." I urged.

"I'm not staying out here in the sun." Doug argued logically.

As soon as he slid open the door, Titan pounced, clambering up him, kissing him and grunting endearments. Doug was quite taken aback, having been braced for battle, at this sudden reversal of roles.

Titan walked him to his chair, still holding his hand, looking up into his face with sycophantic adulation. As soon as he was seated, he rushed to untie his shoe-laces and helped remove his shoes, looking around for his sandals. I fetched them both a coca cola and when I came into the room, Doug was reading his paper and Titan sat beside him similarly occupied.

When he deemed Doug suitably revived, he initiated a game of Patter-cake, which Eddie Brewer had taught him and lead on to more boisterous games. Until Doug was swinging him by the arms and running around the room with Titan on his shoulders, exactly how I had imagined they would be together.

Landing was quite puzzled when he returned that Titan had not rushed out to greet him and came into the room nodding his head approvingly in their direction as they romped and finished their cokes.

"Titan like dee master, Ha ha!" was his repeated theme in the kitchen that evening.

Nobody measured up to Titan's new-found hero, even Landing had to take second place. Titan anticipated Doug's presence eagerly, merely tolerating us whilst he was away at work. With his newly-found measure of respect, Titan obeyed Doug obsequiously, without him even having to raise his voice.

I fear I never rose to such revered heights and he continued just as retractable once he was with me. Having sat for hours under a tree Titan was obstinately reclined in one 'mad-dogs and Englishwomen' sort of afternoon, I was feeling tempted to throw a Titan-type tantrum myself.

A scorching Harmattan wind blew directly off the Sahara and he had escaped on the way back from a long morning walk, when I was already exhausted, parched and hungry.

Arriving home to find the house empty and doors ajar, Doug had surmised the familiar situation and came in search of the errant ape. As I rushed up to tell him my self-pitying story, Titan came down and rushing to his idol, interjected.

"Oo-Oooh! Oo-Oooh!" pointing to me as if to say I told a pack of lies. He climbed lovingly into Doug's arms, proffering kisses and chattering in short staccato grunts and every so often looking back towards me with a long drawn "Oooooooh!"

"Oo-Oooo! Oo-Oooo!" I ejaculated back at him, I was learning to swear in Chimpanzee!

When I reached home and thankfully sank into a cool bath, I found the scorching wind had burnt a red mark down my back where it had heated my zip. I began to appreciate why there had been no-one else about.

Being unaccustomed to this dry hot wind, we settled by the open window, wondering why Titan stayed in the airless hall until we discovered it was the sensible action to take.

He never attempted the rough and tumble games with me that he instigated with Doug but was gentle and affectionate. He would often pause midst some preoccupation, suddenly aware of my presence in the room and come over to pat me on the shoulders gently or plant an elongated kiss upon my cheek. I accepted this as a loving gesture and glowed under such precious and unique love.

Although it could well have been some form of acknowledgement from a superior towards a subordinate member of the troop!

He would sometimes grab my leg as I passed, having detected some splinter or thorn with his keen eyesight, yanking me to the floor. I was then expected to sit patiently whilst Dr Titan endeavoured to extract it. He was most adept at such ministrations, peering myopically and probing with his sharp finger nails. Should the splinter prove stubborn, he would clench his teeth and whistle on indrawn breath, glancing at me to see if it hurt, then suck the foreign body out.

Titan also groomed Paddy and spared me the tiresome chore of de-ticking him. One can rarely run a hand over a dog in the tropics without encountering the bumps of large ticks, which adhere as imperceptible specks and swell as they feed on the host's blood to the size of a small pea. Titan had something of a phobia about ticks and although he consented to rid Paddy of them, he did so with nothing but revulsion, which was apparent from the disgusted expression on his face. When desperate to retrieve him, I could occasionally convince him that he harboured a dreaded parasite by making a chimp 'danger' call, when he would scurry down anxious for me to relieve him of it, although I only ever once found one on him.

Paddy would reciprocate by 'fleaing' Titan, nibbling him canine fashion, which induced Titan's most convulsive laughter. It would reverberate around the house, sounding like a congested drain-pipe, until he helplessly struggled to sit up to draw breath and cuff away the tears which spilled from the corners of his eyes.

Now that Doug was such a respected figure in his life, Titan lived in dread of offending him. Whilst Doug was having a bath one afternoon, Titan had been amusing himself by drawing the huge curtains across the picture windows, much to the delight of the crowd at the gate. Then to his horror it came down – curtain, runner, plaster and all! He was not to know that it was already insecure and had fallen down before. He crawled out from beneath the curtain and attempted to lift the heavy runner without success. He bit his lip, looking up to where it had been situated and ran his finger through the chalky plaster dust.

Titan's convulsive laughter would reverberate around the house

He then suffered the most uncomfortable fifteen minutes I ever witnessed, as he paced the room, edging open the door to look out for Doug from time to time. His apprehension was only too apparent from his mannerisms and he rushed over to grab my arm, fingering it agitatedly as he heard Doug emerging from the bathroom. We were so amused at his reaction, that he did not receive the reprimand he had anticipated, even better, he was able to assist in putting the curtain runner back up. His face visibly lightened when the most coveted object in the house was produced – the drill, which was normally prudently locked away from Titan. He climbed up the step-ladder with Doug, his head so close to the drill to obscure Doug's view. It gladdened my heart to see them working together, as Doug asked him to hand him the bit. I wondered whether I could not find a few more weekend chores for them to tackle!

It was becoming apparent that Landing needed some assistance, trekking around with Titan in the heat of the day, anticipating his every need and finishing his housework late at night. He was a frail-looking man at best, but was becoming positively skeletal as indeed was I! He would set out for his long cycle-ride home appearing so worn and jaded, still insisting, 'It is my work' with a martyred air. I felt more tyrannical than ever.

There appeared some misunderstanding, as word passed around the area that we were in need of a nanny. Neat, capable-looking maidens appeared bearing testimonials as to their accomplishments in child-care, only to make the hastiest of exits on being confronted by my cavorting chimp. Not that Titan gave them much chance, as he apparently felt obliged to intimidate all young females and their subsequent screaming had the most unfortunate effect upon him. He leapt up and down flailing his long arms, shouting his objections after their rapidly retreating forms.

I fear Fatou suffered mercilessly at Titan's hands. A shapely girl of ample proportions, who walked around the house topless as Titan sauntered after her. I would soon hear Fatou cautioning,

"Titan, no, no. Titan no! Stop it" as her voice built up to a state of screaming hysteria until she came fleeing through the house wearing nothing but a pair of brief panties, with Titan bounding in her wake, a rakish leer upon his face, waving her wrap-around skirt

Fatou came running through the house wearing nothing but a brief pair of panties

triumphantly. The highlight of her thrice-weekly visit, as far as Titan was concerned, was to intimidate and dis-robe the unfortunate girl. Landing, who also bullied Fatou from the moment she stepped in the door, did nothing to discourage Titan's sport and in fact he revelled in Fatou's predicament, to a point where it actually induced an unaccustomed smile on Landing's tragic countenance.

The selection of Titan's new retainer, therefore, had to rest solely with him and he continued to conduct interviews throughout the following weeks. He reacted so violently to the majority of the applicants that I began to despair of the post ever being filled.

For Titan's choice of friends were dubious to say the least although through him I met some delightful characters I should not otherwise have known, of sub-normal intellect, or as Landing described them, 'Not so right for dee 'ead!'

One of the few people we encountered on our daily walks was a cheerful, rotund lad, whom I called the Cherub. He was always occupied ineptly weaving dried grasses, insisting he was making baskets and hats. Titan would approach him with gentle affection, putting an arm around his shoulder and studying the tangled mess at which he worked. Titan would scratch his chin thoughtfully and sometimes endeavour to assist. I had been quite startled when we first encountered him, but he merely greeted us brightly calling:

"Ello lady, ello monkey, ello doggie." As if accustomed to meeting such a trio in the deserted mangrove swamps.

"I make you fine hat monkey." He would promise Titan and there was a definite bond between them.

Ebrima constantly shadowed us, a sombre, gangling lad with long matchstick legs and neck. I felt it tactful to ignore him, but Titan would run back to reveal Ebrima's ineffective hiding places, as he stalked us, re-enacting the theme of the current local film. Many was the Arabian epic replayed, as Ebrima's head emerged from behind a sand-dune on the beach or the gangster chase or cowboy quick-draw as he darted from tree to tree.

The willowy shadow appeared on our veranda daily as his fatuous voice boomed in,

"Daw, I come beg one cigarette madam." Sounding so like the Goon Show's Eccles, that I could barely believe he had not been modelled on Titan's lanky friend. Ebrima running was the strangest sight of all and I could only liken it to a galloping giraffe, as he loped on gangling legs, his neck and body swaying cumbersomely.

I doubt that I ever managed a solitary walk along the beach, without returning to find giant footprints interspersed with my own and it was not difficult to guess who 'Man Friday' was. I was one day though to be thankful for his shadowing tactics.

Titan was always delighted to see the more ostentatious simpletons that called with their begging tins on Fridays. Particularly one that came to dance and incantate in the driveway in a splendidly primitive fashion, prompting Titan to imitate his weird ritual and place some pennies in the man's cocoa tin.

"Thank you sir, you are a gentleman" he would say, raising his hat to Titan.

I began to fear that I should have no choice but to employ the fatuous Ebrima, the basket-weaving Cherub or one of the deranged beggars to meet Titan's approval.

Eventually, a reticent, wistful old man appeared. He wore a long pair of faded football shorts, a moth-eaten pullover and a large, tatty pair of plimsoles. He was laden with *ju-ju* amulets and had an indefinable musky odour about him, similar to embrocation. He explained he had not been employed for many years, but as he now had a new, young wife and a baby was soon expected, he was forced to seek employment.

His name was Sangyang and apparently had the special aura about him that met with Titan's approval. He smiled benignly at Titan, scooping him up in his arms tenderly, as if he were a fragile, newly-born baby. Titan responded, docile and demure, gazing into the old man's face and fingering his grey hair. Although Sangyang was never to command the high degree of obedience Landing wielded, he could always induce a calming influence over Titan. He could be undergoing one of his more spectacular rages, only to become instantly mollified when Sangyang appeared.

I fear Sangyang indulged Titan even more than Landing, insisting on maintaining a constant vigil over him when he was in his cage. I would urge him to leave and go home, but the old man could not be persuaded to do anything so heartless. He would rise and start to take a few hesitant steps, only to rush back at Titan's slightest demur, to placate his cherished charge. He would still be sitting outside the cage in the garden until long after dark. I had never before seen Titan so much as close his eyes during the day, until Pa Sangyang came. I would often find them mid afternoon, arms entwined around each other and faces pressed together, both soundly sleeping.

I suppose with Titan in residence it was rather reckless of me to even consider having a drinks party, but since Pa Sangyang's demulcent effect upon him and under his constant supervision, Titan had been a reformed character.

It started later than the prescribed cocktail hour, as I had hoped that Titan might have been well settled down for the night. As if he would miss anything as exciting as a party! Sensing some impending highlight, Titan had watched the preparations throughout the day and sat at his window, nothing but wide awake and eager as the first guests began to appear. As people overspilt onto the back veranda, they could hardly fail to notice him and some naturally drifted over to cluster around his cage. Above the party babble, I was aware of sporadic outbursts of the most riotous laughter from that corner of the garden, accompanied by Titan's inimitable guffaws. He was obviously on good form, I thought and keeping everyone entertained.

As guests came in for their glasses to be refilled, they commented

"What a darling, he gave me such a big kiss."

"He pinched Charlie's glasses and put them on himself."

"He's got my handkerchief."

"He looks just like my mother-in-law," said one wag, unoriginally.

Apart from the lady's handkerchief, he appeared to be behaving and I even found myself speculating what an asset a chimpanzee can be in getting a potentially stuffy party warmed up, and I was far too occupied to get a chance to go and look at him myself. Landing, who was supposed to be helping me, was standing at the door welcoming people in and assisting them to park their cars, more in the role of host, if anything. Sangyang, looking rather weird in one of Landing's cast-off uniforms, was so bemused by the whole affair, that he stood midst the chattering throng like a smiling guest. As always, Doug seemed to have disappeared.

When a fresh commotion erupted from the kitchen, I was unable to attract either Landing's or Sangyang's attention and Doug, as usual, was giving an astronomical lecture with his telescope at the bottom of the garden. A trouble-maker had arrived through the back door and been given food, as was customary and had set about fighting KJ who was coping with the washing-up. I foolhardily rushed between them, sustaining punches from both opponents' fists, but was fortunate enough to catch the attention of a young rugby playing guest, who promptly evicted our gate crasher. What with acting as referee in a kitchen brawl, serving drinks and small *chop*, I completely forgot Titan's existence.

As people began to leave and I had a breathing space, I thought to look over towards Titan's party. It still appeared to be in full swing, and I could see his ghoulish silhouette teetering around on his perch most unsteadily and after several precarious lurches, followed by a chorus of gasps from his audience, he toppled to the ground.

"Do you know your chimp's really plastered out there?" Someone told me as they left, still laughing.

I rushed over and found him struggling to get to his feet, only to collapse onto his back, rolly-pollying around with laughter. I lifted him into his sleeping quarters several times but he kept lumbering out again, rheumy-eyed and with an imbecilic leer upon his face, staggered back towards his onlookers, arms outstretched, lips puckered, to embrace and kiss all his friends. He positively loved everybody that night and I suppose he was at least a happy drunk.

"What you let him drink? He's drunk." Landing was horrified when he came over from seeing the last guests out. Being a strict tee-totaller Moslem, nothing was more iniquitous to his mind. He brought large quantities of black coffee to sober up the inebriated ape.

I did not feel it was so much the quantity he had imbibed as the varied mixture, for as fond as he was of spirits he was too sophisticated to take more than the requisite sip, though I dreaded to consider the number of sips he must have taken. It was the only occasion I ever knew him to oversleep, when I went into him in the morning quite late and shook his lifeless form.

"He's dead!" I screamed.

"Where, what?" Landing and Sangyang came panicking over.

We picked him up and shook him, until a red-rimmed eye reluctantly opened, only to promptly shut. Lifting his head appeared a most painful process as he squinted from face to face, as if not quite able to place who we were and our shouting was obviously having the most excruciating effect upon him. He really did have a humdinger of a hangover!

We dosed him with aspirin and strong tea, but he remained in his cage most of the day, laying supine in his darkened sleeping quarters with his hands clutching his head. It was the only day that we never took him out.

Despite Landing's dissensions that Sangyang was inferior

"Dis 'ole man na so strong, he na see so good" Sangyang continued to accompany me on our daily trek.

Whatever deficiency Sangyang's eyesight lacked, Titan's could always be relied upon and he would promptly hoot in alarm at the least danger, drawing my attention to many an obscure snake. I was often wary, however, when he poked his arm, somewhat indiscriminately into crevices of tree trunks but nothing more lethal than a startled owl ever emerged, rotating its head and blinking surprise at the daylight intrusion.

The wide expanse of beach gradually held no terror for Titan, he was even venturing into the sea up to his waist, delighting in defying the huge, oncoming waves. He would collect shells and flotsam and use large pieces of driftwood to pole-vault the advancing sea. He would lean over Paddy, as the latter dug for crabs, peering myopically and getting covered in sand. He was pinched, more than once, as he poked his fingers in the burrows by a protractile claw.

The numerous and giant species of crabs that honeycombed our territory were the only creatures that filled me with horror. It had been something of a trauma when I first took Paddy for a nocturnal walk. I had been puzzled by the clanging and shuffling around me and when I shone my torch and discovered I was wading in a moving mosaic of giant crabs, ebbing at my approach, I fled back home. During the rains when their subterranean homes were flooded the large land crabs would climb up the outside of the mosquito screens. Their protracted eyes and waving claws appeared to me utterly grotesque and it is the one creature that leaves me frozen with illogical horror. I prefer the type of crab that comes out of a tin, fully dressed!

Paddy was a skilful fisherman, as many Labradors are, and Titan would watch fascinated as he brought his catch to the shore and ate it. It was not long before he too began to pick tentatively at the flesh and share Paddy's raw fish with him.

We daily passed the local women who dug for oysters in the tidal pools and having studied their activities for some time, Titan began to probe beneath the water, using both hands and feet. I would take his catch and boil them for him and he added yet another item to his unnatural diet. I pondered how strangely his foraging skills extended those of wild chimps.

It was as well he had overcome his essentially innate fear of water when one day we could so well have drowned him. On returning along a sandy reef we had underestimated the turn of the tide and were nearly cut off. On crossing a narrow tidal stream we were instantly submerged out of our depth. Landing was carrying Titan who would otherwise, I am sure, have taken a sounding for us. As I surfaced I saw Titan struggling on top of Landing's submerged head and his ancient bowler floating past. Before going down for a second time, Landing struggled to say something but all I could make out were gargling cries before he glug-glugged down again. I swam over and managed to support Landing with one hand and paddle with the other, as Titan clutched at us both in screaming terror. From the bubbles that Landing was emitting, I took it that even whilst drowning, he could not be silenced!

My instinctive fear was the knowledge that chimps cannot swim and assumed that was what Landing was trying to impart.

By some miracle we managed to get across against the current onto a shallow ledge. Poor Landing collapsed on his face, spluttering out mouthfuls of water, still trying to speak, whilst Titan leapt and danced gleefully, appearing quite exhilarated by his narrow escape, whilst I chased after and rescued one soggy, black, bowler hat.

At last Landing revived enough to sit up and gasp,

"Please, Madam. I no *savvy* to swim."

I had not been aware of this and knew it could not have been my efforts alone that had driven us across. Landing assured me it had not been him and that Titan had been making swimming motions with his long, powerful arms.

We were indeed a bedraggled trio, and seeing it was the quickest route we walked along the road home, just as a ladies' pukka coffee morning was breaking up and we received the most incredulous stares. They must have concluded we had taken an impromptu bathe, fully dressed.

Titan had soon made it clear that he liked to keep his own spending money and it was apparent that he was fully aware of the bargaining value of his coins. The stories I had been told of him going to market were probably quite valid, as he would offer coins to the traders that called at the house. If they did not hand him the object he wished to purchase, he would offer another, but only up to a point. The vendors of fruit really enjoyed haggling with him, but would always generously throw in a 'dash' before they left.

Titan kept his pennies tied in a handkerchief, the way he had seen Mauritanians keep their cash and like a miser he would often untie them and shuffle through his small change, before tying them up and placing them in his box.

Despite our regular inspections of Titan's cage, he continued to make the occasional break-out. Not so much seeking freedom, I am sure, but more out of a sense of challenge. When unattended I would often catch him working furtively on some portion of the cage, only to leave it when he realised he was observed. He would work at unwinding overlapping wire at odd moments until an unguarded opportunity to abscond. Regrettably for him, I developed a telepathic intuition and would awaken with a jolt in the certain knowledge that Titan was out. I would run to alert Landing, who unconvinced would assure me he had just handed him his morning tea. Sure enough, we would find the cage empty but he was now easily retrieved and soon came bounding in the kitchen door not wishing to miss the days' excursion.

During his time with us he had grown at an alarming rate and his features had begun to change. He looked more like a maturing gorilla than the appealing young chimpanzee, his head appeared flatter and his face had darkened, not to mention his muscular growth. Like anyone who has ever kept a chimp, I knew the time was fast approaching when I would have to part with him, but alas it came unexpectedly and too soon.

The most significant change had been after he shed his milk teeth and he grew large upper canines. One only had to watch him tear through the large fibrous monkey bread kernals from the *boabab* trees to appreciate the strength of his new teeth. When he bit a visitor he inflicted a large ripping wound and we had no alternative than to part with him fairly quickly.

I soon realised my dream of releasing him was not feasible unless I was prepared to live out in the bush with him indefinitely or else banish him to a solitary wild existence. The Gambia being a small country, it would be difficult to find anywhere suitable far enough from habitation and once a wild animal has been tamed, it would always gravitate towards people. Having lost his fear of man, he would remain a potential danger.

Cyril Grace of Dudley Zoo cabled that he would be willing to accept him, even though Titan had passed the age when he would be of much appeal to the public. Unfortunately, we were not able to persuade the airline to accept him unaccompanied, as regulations were tightening up on the indiscriminate exportation of wildlife at that time.

The three-week reprieve passed incredibly fast and there was no alternative than for him to go to a small zoo in *Dakar* in neighbouring Senegal. I was devastated that I had done little to change his fate. I did take comfort that he at least stayed in Africa and I hoped that the lucrative chimp trade, so reminiscent of slavery, had declined.

* * * * * * * *

CHAPTER V
PADDY AND FRIENDS

I was desolate without Titan, as life reverted to its orderly pattern. It was so tempting to purchase one of the many animals that were hawked around the houses, if only to rescue them from their mercenary handlers, but I realised that once money changed hands, every enterprising layabout would see himself as an animal catcher, in the hope of making an easy pound or two. Instead, I urged them to take their captives to Mr Brewer for release in *Abuko*.

Since I had purchased Titan, bush telegraph must have travelled rapidly over the borders, for several small chimpanzees had been diverted into The Gambia for sale, rather than Europe as had been the case. I guessed I had probably overpaid his market value, giving the impression that philanthropic Europeans in The Gambia were a ready market for chimpanzees. The Brewer family now had one of the recent arrivals who they named William, a pathetic emaciated infant that had suffered in his capture and subsequent handling. The Gambian Government promptly legislated against their importation and any that came in were confiscated by the Police.

Landing had often mentioned, *ad nauseum* in fact, Paddy's mother and how he had witnessed Paddy's birth. For like Landing, Paddy had more or less come with the house. So not unnaturally, Landing tended to regard him as his own dog who he allowed to visit us to fuss over and admire. He would ask me, most graciously, every couple of weeks if I would mind taking Paddy to the sheep dip for him. The ill-fated Landing had taken home so many puppies and despite his usual diligence, which he instilled in his dog-loving sons, each in turn failed to survive.

As I learned more of my inauspicious retainer, it was not difficult to understand why he possessed such a grief-stricken face. The poor man was constantly resigned to the next inevitable fall of the axe.

For this reason, he took extra pride in Paddy and basked in the popularity he enjoyed locally. As with black cats in Britain, in Gambian superstition, black dogs augured well. This was fortuitous, as his shortcomings in the village tended to be more readily overlooked, than less favoured canine colours. It was unfortunate that in a society where a man's wealth was judged by his livestock, that Paddy should be a persistent worrier of sheep and goats. I was often summoned to the village urgently by one of Paddy's innumerable friends, though on the first occasion I had been rather puzzled, as it sounded as if he was saying,

"Come, quick quick, missus, Paddy go catch ships."

I would arrive on the scene to find an enraged owner brandishing a machete at the rapacious dog attacking his flock of sheep.

Before Titan arrived, we had seen very little of Paddy, apart from him popping in for the odd meal and much needed bath. He spent most of his days in the village, usually around the abattoir or out hunting with a pack of pye dogs. Any parties held within a three-mile radius, Paddy would be sure to attend and friends would tell us that he had been there. Most nights he spent with an old night-watchman whom he appeared to really adore, and who, no doubt, shared his supper with him. I would see the old man pass and he would call out and wave as he went to and fro. Paddy would be trotting at his heels devotedly, sometimes deigning to throw a glance of recognition in our direction. When he did return, he usually brought home some trophy which he left on the veranda, horns, hooves, a piece of turtle shell and once, even a drowned cat. How he came by such trophies, I did not dare contemplate.

Not long after Titan's departure we found a baboon in the garden. It wore a collar and was obviously an escaped pet, but it was quite unapproachable and did not appear to have gained much trust of homo-sapiens during its captivity. I tried to catch it to remove the collar and take it to *Abuko* but it would not let me come near. I made a nostalgic pursuit through the same gardens where I had pursued Titan, making the same explanations to the occupiers. It made off and we thought no more about it.

The following morning, Paddy's watchman friend called in to tell me that Paddy and his friend Carlos had been chasing a baboon down near the beach. I took it to be no more than a friendly chase, similar to the games he had played with Titan, until he presented me with one of his more grisly trophies.

I had been sunbathing on the beach, whilst Paddy was swimming, when I felt him come over to press something into my hand.

"Good dog." I patted him drowsily, thinking it to be nothing more gruesome than a piece of driftwood. When I did rouse myself I discovered I was clutching a small, black hand! The story of 'the Monkey's Paw' flashed into my mind and I instantly flung it into the sea, scolding the bewildered dog. He who had been an ape's best chum, yet killed a baboon?

"My teacher would really have loved that monkey's hand." Baba complained when I related Paddy's latest escapade and I felt she never really forgave me for parting with such a splendid biological specimen.

Paddy was frequently in scrapes and common to his species, could not be deterred from chasing anything that moved. We had noticed Paddy lying in the garden when we went out one particularly hot evening and were surprised on our return some hours later to find him in the same spot. When I went over to him, I barely recognised him, his head was grotesquely swollen and he was unconscious. On carrying him into the house it was not difficult to surmise he had encountered a spitting cobra and from his state of unconsciousness, he had obviously been bitten too. I remembered reading that cobra venom should be swilled out of the eyes with liquid, but what? For some illogical reason I decided upon milk, which I continued to pour into his eyes for most of the night. The second lid had come down and his eyes were so hideously swollen, it appeared to have little effect, other than to drench his coat and to smell most rancid in the heat.

By morning Paddy was regaining consciousness, to my relief, but his eyes remained swollen and sealed. Not at all daunted, Paddy got to his feet and staggered around blindly, bumping into windows and chairs. On hearing his watchman friend passing and calling,

"Hello Paddy, where you go last night?" he gravitated towards the voice and would have bounded out of the door had I not restrained him. The old man was indeed alarmed when he saw his canine friend and did nothing to alleviate my concern.

"He go meet dis bad snake." He said. "Oh ma poor Paddy boy. Na small time he get sick for dee 'ead. One man go for dee bush, go meet dis bad snake, ee na see no more."

"What happened?" I was foolish enough to ask.

"Den he bite all dee people, before ee go die."

He shook his head mournfully, giving Paddy a rather permanent farewell pat.

He left me little comforted but I felt he might well be confusing cobra blindness with rabies, or even some obscure Ninkey Nanker about which I had not heard.

I sought out my young friend Dembo who was very fond of animals and possessed a great deal of practical knowledge about them. He said his eyes should have been washed out with salt water and went at once to fetch some from the obvious source. There I had been with the Atlantic Ocean lashing on my doorstep and all I had thought to use was precious, imported, long-life milk. Although I had remembered an old African man once telling me of the first aid remedy for cobra blindness was to urinate into the patient's eyes, which left me hoping I should never need such treatment! I daresay out in the bush where there is no other available liquid it is a most practical course, but living on the coast, sea water was far more refined.

Dembo soon had a slit of Paddy's amber eye open as the white film receded he continued to swill with salt water. Having regained this limited vision, there was no holding the intrepid dog, who was anxious to be away and about his daily activities.

It was a week before the lumps subsided, but far longer before his watchman friend could be convinced he was in no danger of running amok foaming at the mouth!

Having spent so much time watching Titan swinging in trees and even venturing up after him a little way, Paddy must have over-estimated his own aerial capabilities when he decided to leap off of the Foon's roof. We had all gone up there to enjoy the maximum Atlantic breeze and as Marion pointed out her flourishing coconut tree to me, I saw Paddy disappear over the side of the roof out of the corner of my eye.

"Is is there a ledge down there?" I asked her, not daring to look over the side.

Paddy jumped off the roof

"Eh no." she said, "Why?"

"Paddy just jumped over." I quavered.

We all peered down, by which time their dog Weedy was barking excitedly and to our relief and amazement, Paddy was struggling to his feet and shaking himself. He looked up at us, as if puzzled at his sudden ejection to ground level. He fortunately suffered nothing worse than a few broken front teeth.

Paddy must have had at least nine lives and we never knew what to expect when he returned from one of his longer treks. Particularly when he waddled in one day, looking most woe-begone with a gait reminiscent of John Wayne, having spent too long in the saddle! We took some time before realising the problem was in the 'doggyhood' region. My staff were most embarrassed and disappeared leaving me to explain to the vet. He said it was a quite common occurrence to experience a fixed erection after copulation and he soon unfixed it.

The vet had actually presumed that Paddy had mated one of the local bitches but this was unlikely. Early on in our acquaintance I had realised that Paddy was gay. He was at least in a permanent relationship with his good mate Carlos. They were inseparable and shared all their exploits. It was at times a source of embarrassment, particularly on one occasion when I was walking down the road with a priest, only to encounter Paddy and friend in the middle of the road coitally joined back to back. I had hoped the Father would not notice but he stopped to regard them commenting "I didn't know they did that."

I fear I was a Judas and did not acknowledge least recognition.

Paddy was delighted when he found a new occupant in Titan's cage, although it bore little resemblance to Titan. It was a young Maxwell's Duiker, a frail fawn that tottered on fragile legs. Paddy, with his aversion to sheep and goats, was nevertheless besotted with her. He went into the cage and licked and nuzzled her and generally acted as surrogate mother in all but one respect. When she sought the teats she was sure he possessed, he would bound away from her in disgust.

Not being the brightest of animals, he anticipated her coming for walks with us and would rush back to the cage when we set out for the beach. He would also gaze expectantly from the inanimate fawn up to Titan's swinging ropes, hoping she might possess some of Titan's acrobatic prowess.

Sadly we lost her, with the bewildering suddenness that wild animals die, with little warning of their even ailing. Young antelopes are very difficult to rear and we wondered whether our formula had been too rich. Paddy was extremely distressed and nudged and licked her lifeless form and yet by the following day, he was paradoxically pestering sheep and goats.

When a herd of goats meandered down the road grazing slowly past, Paddy was immediately in pursuit and there was soon something of a stampede. Foolhardily, I joined the chase, which took us right along the beach, through swamps, scrub and cultivated plots. I yelled, Paddy barked and the goats bleated and things became generally chaotic. When I did eventually grab Paddy by the collar, the goats turned on us. One particularly large virile Ram, butted me into a thorny bush and as I picked myself up, I saw Paddy flying through the air. Paddy sought revenge and the chase continued for an hour or so, eventually taking us back in a homeward direction. Rather than turn in our own gateway, Paddy decided to round them up into our next-door neighbour's garden, who promptly came out to shoo them off. As I came hobbling behind, scratched and torn, she appeared to hold me entirely responsible, as if I chose to spend my afternoons chasing around the countryside with a herd of village goats. I wondered why it was that these slapstick performances always seemed to occur in the heat of the afternoon, whilst more sensible folk had their siesta or rested in the cool of their houses.

Being so closely involved with village life, Paddy also embraced the Moslem faith. When the *Imam* called the faithful to prayer on a Friday, Paddy was one of the first to appear, the mosque being situated conveniently close to the abattoir! He would join the large gatherings of the devout, a small black form conspicuous among the white robes. If he encountered anyone praying on the beach at sunset, he would always go over and join them, moving from a sitting to a laying position, simulating their praying movements.

* * * * * * * *

CHAPTER 6
THE BUSHBABIES

Paddy was not in the least taken with our next guests, who were a pair of bushbaby infants. Apart from displaying an initial disgusted incredulity at their invasion of the house, he endeavoured to avoid them. He reverted to merely dropping in for the occasional meal but only when he was certain that the "flying mice" as he appeared to view them, were not around.

The young twin bushbabies had been found clinging together when a tree was felled and somebody had started to rear them before going on leave and we agreed to care for them while they were away. I was told that they would be perfectly happy nestling down the neck of my dress during the day. I am afraid at first, I recoiled at the touch of their cold, clammy feet and hands scampering up my arm and they were so small and mouselike I felt they might have to seek an alternative nesting site.

Doug, however, seemed quite enamoured of them and was delighted when they dived under his shirt and scampered around beneath it, circumnavigating the friendly giant undulating bulges flatulating about beneath his shirt. Their heads popped out from time to time to regard his face from beneath his sleeves and above his collar.

"I can entertain them without even getting out of my chair" he said, "not as strenuous as swinging Titan around."

"Not as good for the waistline though." I cautioned, having noticed his had thickened again considerably since Titan had left. His daily physical jerks, as he swung Titan around, ring-a-roseying with him and bouncing him from floor to ceiling by the hands had been most beneficial to his waistline.

Unfortunately, his friendship with the bushbabies came to an abrupt conclusion when Doug gave a prodigious sneeze, which must have had the force of an erupting volcano to the Lilliputian creatures.

"Oh dear!" I cried. "Is it your allergy?"

"Must be allergic to theb." He spluttered, as he reached for a handkerchief, before convulsing under a volley of momentous sneezes.

The two young primates who normally appeared to be in a permanent state of bewildered astonishment, fled onto the top of the wardrobe, until it seemed their large, bulbous eyes would pop right out of their heads. They clung together, their heads turning in clockwork precision, looking more astounded by the minute. They remained very wary of Doug after that, and he would only have to produce a handkerchief to set them scuttling off.

I purchased a large paw-paw, which Titan would have devoured in minutes, only to get them to accept the tiniest morsel each, fruit and a food supplement making up their diet at that stage. I had been told they were fed at hourly intervals during the day, but it would often take me that length of time to locate them for a feed. It appeared most careless to mislay two entire primates but they never settled in the same place twice and were able to conceal themselves in the most unlikely places. They would crawl into the linings of curtains, unnoticeably hidden in a fold, behind pictures and inside vases.

Landing's reaction to them had been much the same as Paddy's, after displaying horrified surprise that they were to have the run of the house and not be kept in a small hutch in the garden, he pretended they did not exist. He could not be convinced that they were anything other than small rodents that he insisted we would soon be overrun with, even when I showed him their hands, which had four long tapering fingers and a thumb. I suppose catering to a couple of twin mice hardly held the same prestige as controlling a large ape.

"Landing, could you please help me find the bushbabies, I've lost them again." I would call him from the kitchen.

"Eh, em!" he would scoff. "Make I call the carpenter, he make small box for them to stay. One master have piccans keep dese t'ings, they get small house with wheel, when they run dee wheel move."

"I've looked in all the curtains, they're not in there."

Landing proceeded to smell his way around the house, certain he was able to sniff them out.

"They get small bit stink" he insisted.

"Her-hum!" I heard him exclaiming from the bedroom.

"Have you found them?" I called.

"Her-hum!" he repeated.

I found him standing in the bedroom doorway inclining his head towards the dressing table.

"Where?" I could not see them, but he kept on inclining his head and 'her-humming' in that direction. I eventually spotted them underneath a ridge at the back of the mirror.

"Can you just stay there please Landing and make sure they don't move, while I get their *chop*." But he just walked back into the kitchen muttering 'Dey get small bit stink' and wiping imaginary marks from the walls as he went, with his carbolic-soaked cloth.

Sangyang revealed nothing of Landing's revulsion to my small *galagoes*. Although they aroused none of the protective affection Titan had, he tended more to humour me with my new pets. He would stand smiling benignly as I fed them or they leapt around the room. It could, of course, just have been the natural benevolent expression he always wore, whereas Landing's was a natural scowl. Without Titan there was not very much for the old man to do and I did not want to sack him, as he was not really likely to find other work. I fear he did get somewhat under Landing's feet, so I appointed him Head Bushbaby Keeper, which seemed to please him. So he sat there with them whilst they slept all day.

I decided we should have to restrict them to the spare room, at least during the day, when they tucked themselves away for a good day's sleep. Landing was delighted with this news, and nodded his head sagely, indicating that he knew I would eventually see sense. However, he did not look quite so delighted when he saw Pa Sangyang gathering and bringing in branches, foliage and buckets of sand.

I was very pleased with the effect when Sangyang and I had completed our conversion. I had modelled it on the Charles Clore Pavillion at Regents Park of course and one would hardly know it had ever been a bedroom. An ideal environment for bushbabies!

"What do you think?" I asked Landing when he came in to see what we had been up to, I knew his curiosity would overcome his disgust.

"Dat my best bucket" he said, taking my largest central tree away.

It was unfortunate that Doug should bring home an official Housing Inspector that evening, who was visiting The Gambia to look at post-hiring properties. It all went well, I managed to show him around leaving the bushbabies' door shut and I did not think he noticed that we had missed a room but then Baba came bounding in.

"Can we see the bushbabies?"

"Bushbabies eh!" The inspector seemed quite interested and Baba led the way.

He did not actually see them, as they would never come out whilst strangers were around and his face betrayed very little as he glanced at the miniature jungle I had just created. He made no comment at all, but from the stories he told, it appeared he encountered the most peculiar things in the course of his duties and I guessed he would be adding our boxroom to his list of bizarre anecdotes.

As the bushbabies had appeared so indistinguishable at first, I called them Bill and Ben, after the television Flower-Pot Men – 'Was it Bill or was it Ben?' I would croon to them. When a friendly head appeared in response to my call, it did not take me long to decide that was Bill, who had a far more amiable and adventurous disposition than his timid, unsociable brother. Bill soon responded to my squeaky voiced blandishments, plopping onto my shoulder and keen to accept a bite to eat. Ben, on the other hand, would flee from one side of the room to the other, evading the proffered food, until I could corner him and at least force a few drops of the milky mixture down his throat.

When an upper cupboard door had been left open one day, they had discovered a large basket inside which they adopted for their daytime nest. This was very convenient as I could be sure of finding them cuddling up to each other in there when the next mealtime came round.

At dusk, they would begin to stir, Bill being the first to come out of their room to find us and settle on Doug's or my shoulder. He would then return, obviously trying to encourage his retiring brother to come out with him. After an hour or so, Ben would be persuaded, but keeping as close as possible to Bill and as far away from us as he could.

They would then scurry around all evening, along the curtain runners, up the standard lamp, bounding from sideboard to chair in miniature kangaroo-like leaps. Their back legs were proportionately long which gave them great impetus to leap from one side of the room to the other like frogs. A picture would begin to sway upon the wall somewhat precariously, until two peek-a-boo faces bobbed out simultaneously on either side.

Should Paddy appear home at this point, peering in through the window, there was no encouraging him in and he would go away seeking the preferable abode of his night watchman. Even Landing was persuaded to leave at a more reasonable hour of night and was even deterred from 'pumping' the bedrooms, as I insisted it would be lethal to my two small guests.

It appeared luxurious to us to sleep in an unpolluted room again that did not knock us unconscious with insecticide fumes. I was not really aware of any mosquitoes, but Doug gladly suffered the bites he sustained uncomplainingly! We did seem to be getting through inordinately large quantities of carbolic, which Landing appeared to be slopping around more abundantly than ever and muttering about killing germs, which I am sure he felt the bushbabies were riddled with.

Visitors seemed to find the twins' evening activities somewhat disconcerting, as they bounded on and off the dinner table or sat staring like a couple of scandalised, old ladies witnessing an orgy. They did tend to subject strangers to a thorough scrutiny, staring for minutes at a time at an unknown face.

I had become quite fond of Bill, who would happily ride around on my shoulder and nuzzle under my chin affectionately, as he watched whatever I was doing. He enjoyed swinging on my hair and out of sheer desperation, Ben would sometimes join him on his monstrous human perch. Ben was far less refined than his brother and his manners left much to be desired. When I felt warm fluid trickling down my back or a needle sharp tooth take hold of my ear lobe, I had no need to ask "Was it Bill or was it Ben?" For Bill would never behave so uncouthly.

Before retiring it was now a matter of 'softly, softly, catch dee galagoes' to settle them into their room, not quite in the same league as tracking down Titan, but equally frustrating, where Ben was concerned. No sooner had I taken a chair to stand on to pluck him from some lofty perch, when he would promptly bound to the other side of the room, whilst Bill watched his errant brother, turning his head back towards me, as if in apology. I suppose they could well have had the run of the house for the night, but after Titan I became so escape-minded, I imagined anything that came into our care was just waiting for a fractionally opened door or window to get away. I doubt that Ben would have so much as ventured out.

Their games continued right through the night and it was unbelievable that the nocturnal clamour was being produced by merely two minute creatures. It sounded more like a team of noisy burglars devastating the house, and trampling around in clogs at that.

Bill soon flourished and grew whilst his withdrawn, finicky brother remained puny and they could now be identified at a glance just from their size. I still spent a great deal of time pursuing Ben with nutritious morsels but always ended up force-feeding him.

I thought it time that Bill was weaned, as he appeared nearly fully grown and the introduction of living prey might be more to Ben's liking than the slops I had been giving him. I had rather expected them to pounce instinctively on the first insect produced, but this was far from the case.

"Look what I've got for my babies" I cooed, as I produced my surprise from behind my back. I dangled a large, juicy grub before them on the end of my tweezers and they instantly vanished up into their cupboard. They clung together standing on their hind legs, their heads turning as they studied the writhing grub to regard each other questioningly. So petrified did they appear, that I almost expected to hear them scream.

Their weaning was not going to be as easy as I had imagined, but I nonetheless persevered, offering them microscopic portions until Bill came to savour the odd fillet of moth, loin of beetle or grasshopper cutlet, provided it was quite inanimate and not still crawling around.

"Give them Roachcocks" (cockroaches). Landing dismissed the subject when I sought his advice on where best to hunt my miniature game.

Like most tropical houses, at least in The Gambia, ours was infested with cockroaches at night. I quickly learned not to be startled when I suddenly switched on the light and however often we were fumigated, vast armies of them marched out of the plumbing nightly. We would leap around stamping on them, inventing a rather fetching dance rather like a flamenco. I had been puzzled the first night we arrived home late, to see Doug switch on the lights and start cavorting around, as I was closing the garage door. I thought he was emulating the hero of the Kung Fu movie we had just been to see. As plentiful as cockroaches were, however, I did not feel I could inflict them on my fastidious friends.

Pa Sangyang, always anxious to please me, was getting somewhat carried away as he presented me with barrow-loads of foliage every day until the spare room became a veritable jungle, and the local trees were becoming somewhat sparse. I did not like to hurt his feelings or crush his initiative, but my heart began to sink each time I saw an approaching tree staggering under a pair of ancient bandy legs clad in old baggy shorts! I therefore assigned him the new and more interesting task of Insect Hunter although he appeared quite content to spend his afternoons sitting vigilantly outside the spare room door whilst the bushbabies slept, much as he had with Titan.

Baba and Candy appreciated coming to see our latest pets in complete safety though I fear they saw little of them. They were so camouflaged in the lush vegetation festooned around the room and when they did come near, it was only to play in my hair. As they developed it came to be their main preoccupation, burrowing underneath it or swinging on the ends of strands, that Baba and Candy only caught veiled glimpses of them. They became capable of unfurling the most elaborate coiffure, flicking out hair-pins or unwinding a plait, as whatever I tried to deter them failed. Covering it with a scarf was no solution, they soon wriggled beneath it and I had to settle for a unique tangled, messy hairstyle, which pre-dated the 'punk look'.

At the end of the dry season we began to experience plagues of various flying insects, which heralded the rains, when they had already arrived somewhere up-country. After eight months of dry, dusty weather, one suddenly could smell the refreshing moisture wafting in the sticky humid night air. This would be warning of the imminent winged invasion and we normally switched off all the lights, so as not to attract them. As Bill and Ben were beginning to regard meals on wings with less horror and were displaying a definite aptitude at pouncing on decoy marbles and pencils, in play practice, we welcomed the swarm, flooding the house with light.

"Sausage flies" I cried delightedly, as the first one wriggled under the door.

"Just as long as there aren't too many" Doug said with reservations.

"Nonsense, they are most nourishing. I bet all the children in Banjul are out under lamp-posts collecting them in their tins."

"Errrr!" Doug grimaced as he ducked, one zooming over his head as they began to bombard the room.

"Look how the dogs gobble them up, Paddy loves them. For some children up country it must be like the ice cream man calling."

Doug remained unconvinced, as the sausage flies began to catapult off of his reading lamp onto his book.

"Come on den Billy boy, sausage flies for supper." I urged and he bounded out in response. He sat on my shoulder, darting his head as he watched the flying display, as they crashed into the walls, shedding their wings and ended writhing on the floor. He appeared very excited and was out of the door in one bound, rushing to fetch brother Ben. Ben returned with him, quicker than usual, though hopping hesitatingly behind, taking two bounds to Bill's one.

I sat down to watch my growing infants feast on their first abundance of natural fare, but they passed straight through and into the dining room. We heard them scampering and leaping and obviously in an excited state, so I surmised that some flies were making their way in there too.

When I went into the dining room, the object that was holding their frenzied attention was nothing more nutritious than the new bureau that had been delivered that day. They could not have been more pleased if it had been purpose-designed for their games, as they chased each other in and out of the pigeon holes and scurried around the shelves. They remained occupied the entire evening, totally ignoring the tasty flying chipolatas, which I set about sweeping up.

“Sausage flies” Landing greeted me the following morning, displaying a dustpan-full.

“Er, yes.” I said apologetically, as he proceeded to sweep piles of them from under the furniture.

“They go spoil my machine.” He complained. (The vacuum).

“I thought the bushbabies would *chop* them.” I explained.

“Agh!” He coughed, “Dey no eat flies, dey *chop* cheese.” (Still insisting they were mice.)

Pa Sangyang was proving to be an excellent grasshopper catcher but they still appeared frighteningly large to my small *galagoes* and I told him about the large colonies of red ants I had seen in Bakary’s citrus trees. He returned saying that Bakary had chased him away, and nobody was allowed in the compound, so I went along myself.

“I wondered whether I might have some of your ants?” I asked him cautiously, pointing to an ant-infested lemon tree.

“No, dee master say no-one take dese lemonis.” He rushed to stand protectively in front of the tree.

“No, not the fruit, those small thing that *humbug* the tree, these ants.”

“Anjes? Why you want dese? You go *chop* them?” he asked suspiciously.

“No. No.” I laughed. “Not for me, my bushbabies they *chop* anjes, I mean, ants.”

“Babies,” he repeated, “you get *piccans*?”

“No, not *piccans, bush piccans.* Like small monkey with long tail.”

He continued to look perplexed and I was amazed how few Gambians knew about bushbabies as they were quite prolific. This always heartened me, as it bode well for their survival.

“You come to my house and I will show you.” I said.

I suppose I should have known better in view of our past confusing interactions. I took him into the dense interior of the spare room and he ducked under an overhanging branch and gazed around enlightenedly. Obviously taking it to be some strange new fad in European décor.

"Bill and Ben. Bill and Ben." I began to sing in the childishly high voice they had come to associate me with.

"Come on den. Where's my 'ikkle boys." I crooned, as Bakary stepped back nearer the door. It was noon and the time of day they were least inclined to rouse themselves and not so much as one bulbous eye appeared. So, suitably doubled over for them to leap on my back, I began to sing their song.

"Bill and Ben are gonna come out tonight, come out tonight..... and dance by the light of the room." It seemed most appropriate to them and normally brought them leaping and bounding out in a frenzy of excitement – but not at noon it seemed!

By this time Bakary was really eyeing me apprehensively and backing down the hallway.

"Landing will explain" I assured him and called Landing.

"You tell Bakary about the bushbabies and how they eat ants."

From the little I followed of Landing's description, it did little to help and he appeared to be telling him about some flea-infested, smelly vermin we were scourged with that madam deluded herself into believing were some sort of monkey and quite ruining his insecticide regime. I heard Titan's name mentioned several times, accompanied by Landing touching his head and Bakary began to view me more sympathetically. Landing was obviously telling the man I had grieved so much for Titan to the point of becoming unbalanced, only I did not feel he was putting it quite so politely.

With reservations, Bakary agreed to supply me with all the red ants I required in exchange for a couple of cigarettes.

"Anjes for your *piccans.*" He would wryly announce, smiling as if humouring me, as he handed over the jar of darting red ants.

Handling them I discovered was a most painful process, as they quickly scurried up my arms, giving painful nips. I tried to adopt Titan's methods and scoop them up in a wodge and offer them to the bushbabies like candyfloss. I never achieved anything like his expertise and just when I felt I was getting the knack, the bushbabies would not co-operate. Bill would extend a hand warily as if about to take them, only to panic at the last moment and flick the antburger to pieces and jump away.

Bill had recently moved out of their joint basket and moved into one of his own, as if he felt Ben always leaning upon him was getting a little tiresome. I fully expected Ben to merely follow, but he must have been getting more independent, as he stayed alone in the original basket.

Although far more bold, they still liked to snuggle under my dress, particularly if they were alarmed. The rainy season appeared to take them completely by surprise and they had none of the natural tolerance to storms that I felt all wild creatures possessed. At the least clap of thunder they would seek me out and dive down the neck of my dress and during a really violent tropical storm, they barely emerged.

This was their most disconcerting habit, as far as Landing was concerned and one he never became accustomed to. When on bringing in my coffee he noticed two extraneous bulges undulating across my bosom, he gaped open-mouthed. Far worse, when two startled faces popped out on either side of my shoulders, he would sometimes drop the tray.

When we had to return the bushbabies to their owner, I was surprised to find how attached I had become to them with their individual, distinctive personalities. As they had become so tame, I had not envisaged any problem in catching them and as I surmised, Bill readily hopped onto my shoulder at first call of his name. Ben proved difficult to the end, and eluded us as he bounded from room to room, leaping out of reach. Doug only managed to capture him by getting Ben's needle sharp teeth firmly embedded in his hand, which he implacably held onto. It was some minutes before we were able to prize his little finger free. Once more we were to arrive late at a dinner party, with Doug's bandaged finger displayed by way of explanation. I am sure people began to wonder whether he did not don a bandage merely as an excuse for unpunctuality.

"Pierre et Jacques mon cheres." The bushbabies' French owner greeted them when we took them back to him. I had not been told that they already had names. However, contrary to both his English and French names, Ben some time later gave birth to twins.

When two startled faces popped out either side of my shoulders

Before leaping onto me, they would moisten their feet and hands on what I presumed to be glands. On a recent David Attenborough programme on the species, he pointed out that they moisten their hands and feet with urine – did Landing know something that I didn't? Did they really stink small bit?

* * * * * * * *

CHAPTER 7
MONTY

At the time the bushbabies left we were nearly ready to go home on leave. Arrangements were a little more complex than the usual holiday packing and vaccinations, as we were accompanying a chimpanzee.

He was one of the small chimps that had arrived in Banjul market soon after I had Titan. From a few months old he had been reared by a young couple in a Banjul flat. His upbringing had been so similar to that of a human baby, that he fully regarded himself as a little boy, rather than an ape. He had played regularly with small children and so naturally modelled himself upon them. The young lady who had raised him had returned home to England and he was left in the care of servants during the day whilst his foster-father was working. So he began to spend the occasional day with me and I was always a willing chimp sitter.

He could not have been more different than Titan, this demure, sloth-like youngster who barely ever misbehaved. He was the epitome of every auntie's favourite toddler nephew. He would be waiting for me when I drove up to collect him, his button nose completely flattened and large elongated lips splodged against the upper storey window. I would see his lips purse in a joyful, unheard hoot and before I had climbed the stairs, he would be rushing down to jump into my arms. His tiny hands clutched the back of my neck, as I was smothered with welcoming kisses. He was then anxious to be on our way and would tug at my skirt or hand, should I loiter to talk to his retainer.

There was one occasion when Monty had settled himself impatiently in the passenger seat of the car, when a sophisticated waiter from one of the hotels way-layed me, asking if I would take a message to a relative in Bakau. Monty tolerated this unforgivable delay for only so long, until his small hairy arm shot out of the open window landing a left-hook squarely on the young man's chin. I fear the poise of the 'a la mode' city-slicker was rather rudely shattered. As well mannered as Monty was, I soon discovered that he was not beyond giving the old one-two to anyone who derided or laughed at the hirsute *piccan.* This was perfectly understandable, as he fully took his appearance to be that of any normal small boy. As a miniature welter-weight though, he posed little threat as he chose to use his fists, rather than his teeth.

Like most of his human contemporaries, Monty's great passion was cars and he would stand up and 'Oooh' enthusiastically at any unfamiliar models we passed on the road. He loved to inspect the dashboard of strange cars and would run his fingers knowingly along the dials and controls. He hooted urging me to overtake any car ahead and turned to look out of the rear window as we accelerated away from it. He was a far less nerve-wracking passenger than Titan had been, for his main objective had appeared to test the escape-proofing of any car he entered and yank on the choke and gear lever to ascertain whether they came apart.

As I had been told that Monty was frightened of dogs and in view of the baboon episode, I was reluctant to introduce him to Paddy when I first took him home. However, when Paddy saw me emerge from the car with a diminutive hairy toddler tucked under my arm, his obvious delight was such that I did not have the heart to banish him. He approached Monty so gently, imploring him to become his friend that he must have communicated his goodwill and it was not long before Monty extended the back of his hand towards the dog's face.

As Paddy appeared to be anticipating, I took them both down to the beach, Paddy walking to heel, looking up devotedly at his new chimpanzee as I carried him. I lowered Monty onto the sand and Paddy towered above him protectively, whilst Monty patted his head and fingered the medallion on his collar, which certified he had been immunised against rabies. They pottered around the mangroves together, Monty walking bi-pedal holding onto Paddy's collar and when a crab scurried too close, he flung his arms around the dog's neck. Paddy made no attempt to instigate the rowdy games he had enjoyed with Titan and should he become at all rough, Monty curled up into a vulnerable ball, hands across his head, until Paddy licked a mute apology into the chimp's large ear.

On further acquaintance, Monty began to climb on Paddy's back for a ride, clinging on tightly to his collar as Paddy waded into shallow water. Monty looked back towards me, revelling in his daring.

When Doug tried to play the same game that he had with Titan though, taking Monty by the hands to swing him around, he merely froze petrified, with no apparent concept of bouncing from the floor. Similarly, when I attempted to place him in a tree, his face spread in a terrified grimace and he showed no obvious inclination towards an arboreal life. He appeared devoid of all climbing ability, which left me wondering at what young age he had been taken from his mother.

When I handed him a glass of milk, he merely let it slip from his hands and I realised I had taken Titan's accomplishments much for granted, not appreciating they had been learned over the years.

His ponderous, calculated movements did make him a more likely contender for the Soccer Stars' Mascot, as he was no mean dribbler and quite capable of a well-placed pass. He enjoyed several training sessions with the big boys and became one of their devoted supporters.

I had not known of his enthusiasm for football, which accounted for his continued interest in Doug's wardrobe. Not a chimp to take or touch anything unless specifically invited to do so, I had been puzzled to find him inching open the door a fraction and peeping in the wardrobe, hooting in awe on several occasions. His restraint had been remarkable when I discovered that Doug had nothing less than a super Wembley-type football secreted in there for presentation to the winners of the local league. It became the highlight of Monty's visits, when the miniature soccer star was allowed to dribble the large football around the house and garden.

Unlike those harem-scarem days with Titan, we would spend restful afternoons together on the beach, sharing a picnic of mangoes and bananas, whilst Paddy hovered near to hand. The chimp and dog would lie contentedly together under the sunshade, whilst I dozed in the tropical sun. I would then take him in to tea at the Foon's house, which held none of the sparkle of our original chimpanzee tea-party, but was far less disconcerting. Baba would take Monty into her room and let him look through her toys and it was all very civilized. Somehow, Baba did not display quite the same degree of interest in him that she had with Titan, although he was a more predictable playmate, for it was hardly more exciting than having a small, well-behaved toddler visiting.

Having overcome his fear of dogs, he began to regard himself as something of a dog-trainer and would flail his arms hooting masterfully as he ordered the resident dogs around in any house he visited.

His main interest in strange households were not so much the dogs or contents of toy boxes, but the vehicles parked out in the yard. He was truly amazed to find the engine of our neighbour Kebba's VW was in the back, when he discovered Kebba working on it. He climbed over Marion's nifty Mini-moke, unique in The Gambia and stroked young Kebba's motor-bike admiringly.

Riding piggy-back, he would help me to search for the bushbabies, calling out if he spotted them before I did. He watched intrigued as I endeavoured to force some milky food supplement into Ben's reluctant mouth. I later allowed him to hold the spoon and guided his hand as he tipped the contents into Bill's more accessible jaws. He would handle Bill with the fascination of a boy of his age caring for a pet hamster. When the bushbabies came out at dusk to play their nocturnal games, he would settle down on the floor to watch their aeriel antics thoughtfully.

When Monty went to visit William, the Brewer's chimp of a similar age, Monty's reticence was even more obvious. William had recovered from his early ailments and timidity and was now a robust, bounding tomboy. It was difficult to believe he was the same nervous emaciated creature who had been reluctant to even venture out of his box.

We had first noticed the change occurring when we had visited the Brewers' house one afternoon and discovered the family were out. We had stopped to talk to William for a while and petted him, but apart from extending a sinewy arm and peeping out of his box at us, he appeared quite inanimate. Imagine our surprise on bidding him farewell and walking a little way along the road, when somebody called out,

"Hey, your chimp's following you."

We looked around to see William's frail frame, spidering slowly behind us. I remembered it as the turning point in his development and looking at him now with Monty, showing off and prancing around, it was certain that he would never look back.

They were both about two years old, but William's enlightened personality made him appear the elder. His current passion it seemed was dancing and Monty watched bemused as Willie demonstrated his particular disco jive, bouncing on an old camp bed on the veranda.

At this enquiring age I was foolish enough to instruct him in the art of opening zip fasteners, a skill I and many visitors were to rue, but knowing Will, it would only have been a matter of time before he had worked it out for himself. He also loved to squat on the back of my chair and remove the hairclips, clenching the extracted clips in one hand, smacking his lips loudly, as chimps do when they groom each other.

William was very much one of the family and we began to refer to him as Bill Brewer. He would set off with Eddie to work in the Land Rover and generally help supervise forestry matters. He assisted with planting saplings and inspected nursery beds. He was first at the table at mealtimes and insisted on joining Eddie in his bath when they returned from a day's work. Yet despite all this, he still remained essentially a chimpanzee.

Of all the chimps I have known, Monty was the least vocal, apart from an occasional exclamation to draw attention to something that caught his eye. This combined with his ponderous manner, made it difficult not to treat him as the child he obviously considered himself to be. William had made a profound impression upon him, although not apparent at the time, as he was later only too ably display.

Since Monty's owner was no longer able to keep him, he had arranged for him to go to Dudley Zoo and unlike Titan, he was still of an age when he would easily adapt and young enough to be an attraction to the public. The airline agreed to accept him provided he was escorted and we happily agreed to take him with us, when he could spend the overnight stop in our care at Las Palmas. We wrote to the hotel, and were agreeably surprised how readily they accepted. I had no qualms whatsoever about Monty's behaviour, he was so polite and anxious to please, one could have taken him to Buckingham Palace without cause for concern, or so I thought!

Donnie Graham, the vet in The Gambia, recommended a mild tranquillising injection before the flight to ensure he suffered the least apprehension and we would have to administer a booster the following morning before leaving Las Palmas. As I was dubious about my ability to do this, I went along to the village hall where I understood a veterinary clinic was in session. I had been misinformed, as it was mother and baby day but they were most accommodating and offered me a baby's buttock to practise upon! The sister was most crestfallen when I declined, feeling unable to inflict pain on one so small and settled to practising on a grapefruit at home.

Monty objected when Donnie stuck the needle in his posterior and the vet narrowly missed one of his swift left-hooks. He settled down on the way to the airport drowsily, showing no interest in the car ride. Fatou, in whom he had aroused maternal instincts, insisted on seeing him off, had him cradled in her arms, watching over him like a devoted nanny.

When we reached the airport building, which consisted of one unpretentious corrugated iron room, it was more overcrowded than usual for the weekly European flight. Fatou's friends came over to admire her cute, unusual *piccan.*

Awoken by the bustle, Monty catapulted out of Fatou's arms with unaccustomed liveliness. He then proceeded to gallop around the terminal at an alarming pace, jumping onto the Immigration Officer's desk and quite startling the man. He hurled himself at a wall feet first, turning into a backward somersault with an agility he had never formerly revealed.

On taking him into the ladies' toilet he banged on the doors demandingly, before making a forceful exit, leaving me alone to offer explanations when outraged occupants emerged. He then disgraced himself when Fatou picked him up by wetting all over her fine brocade *warrumba* and unwinding the yards of her elaborate matching *tiko* which had swathed her head. We were all flabbergasted by his untypically ebullient behaviour, but attributed it to the unfamiliar clamour of the overcrowded building.

I had rather been hoping that he would be allowed to travel on my lap inside the cabin of the plane; I had even nurtured a wild dream of allowing him to view the cockpit, but of course the airline would not permit it. In any case, the plane was full with end-of-term, homebound teachers and in view of his unusual behaviour, I came to think it was probably as well.

We placed him in his travelling crate and supervised his loading into the hold. It was deafeningly noisy at the rear of the plane where the jets roared but Monty seemed quite unperturbed. I was tense and impatient throughout the flight, conscious of the least turbulence and noise, as I considered Monty below in the hold.

I had managed to get a seat adjacent to the door and was first off when we touched down at Las Palmas and stood waiting for the hold to be opened. Monty was revealed sitting inside his crate, blinking at the sudden surge of sunlight quite unconcerned and sucking on a mango stone. I longed to release him but was told he must remain crated.

The Gambian President, who had been on the plane came over to see him and asked where he was going. I was still nervous about giving the injection to Monty the following morning and much to Doug's consternation, I asked the President if he would be able to do it for me if I had trouble. After all, he was a qualified veterinary surgeon and he did not appear to mind my asking, being a most approachable man.

On the airport bus I was still unable to release Monty from his crate but he did not appear to mind too much, as he had recognised some of 'the other children' he knew from The Gambia and they shared their sweets and talked to him. By the time we reached the hotel though, he was beginning to get a little fractious.

At the hotel desk, our name was immediately connected with a booking for a chimpanzee and a registration form was handed to Doug to complete. Just as his pen hovered, poised to sign the completed form, a supersonic scream rent the air. The clerk snatched back the form from Doug's hand, pointing out, not unreasonably, that they were unable to accept any creature that was likely to cause a disturbance to their other guests. Monty then proceeded to have a sensational tantrum that did full justice to any of Titan's more spectacular ones. It was the first that we had ever known Monty to throw and unfortunate that it should be in the cavernous confines of an old Spanish building, where his shrill screeching echoed incongruously primaeval. Doug assured the clerk that once we released Monty and took him to our room that he would soon be quiet, but the man shook his head adamantly. The hotel manager had appeared on the scene, not surprisingly drawn by the demonic screeches and I thought I detected amongst the torrent of outraged dialogue, the words 'Salvaje Bestia'. It appeared that we and our savage beast were about to be thrown out onto the street.

Doug came over to me grave faced, as I endeavoured to pacify Monty and above the vociferation said,

"It might be better if we go out of sight, so leave him alone, you are only making him worse."

"We can't just walk away" I reasoned

"It always worked with Titan" Doug argued.

So I agreed and much to the horror of the Manager and Clerk, being unable to explain our actions as their English appeared limited, we marched purposefully out of the hotel.

"My goodness, they are just leaving him" we heard somebody queuing at the desk remark.

We waited outside out of sight from Monty until his screams gradually decreased in volume and eventually stopped. The Manager came in search of us, obviously relieved we had not abandoned the savage beast, insisting we take our noisy ape straight to the room and waive the registration formalities until later. I am sure they had misunderstood our actions and thought we were blackmailing them, threatening to leave them to cope with his bestial caprices.

Once installed in our somewhat insalubrious room, we released Monty from his crate and let him explore his surroundings. He really took to hotel life, looking at himself in the mirror and hopefully peering in the wardrobes, lest there be a football tucked away in them. He gave an experimental bounce on the bed and when he went into the bathroom he let forth a delighted exclamation. I went to find out what had taken his fancy and discovered it was the bidet, he was turning on the taps and smelling the sliver of hotel soap as he clambered in, obviously taking it to be a chimpanzee's bath.

We were inundated with young hotel porters aged from ten to fourteen years all anxious to make the acquaintance of the young guest in room 103. I asked one of them if he could kindly purchase some bananas for Monty and said about two kilos would do. The remainder of the boys were promptly evicted when the Manager came in search of them.

As our room was situated adjacent to the kitchen, the Chef called in person to ask if there was anything special the nino would like for dinner. I said I thought a fruit salad and a glass of milk would do nicely and he appeared quite disappointed that he was to prepare nothing more specialised.

The bell boy returned staggering under a load of bananas when I realised I had wrongly assessed the weight of a kilo as it was apparent it was two pounds and not a half. Not that they were wasted, having been out of season for some time in The Gambia, Monty soon ate his way through them and I had to finish his fruit salad myself, as the chef had gone to such pains to produce a mammoth dish for the unique guest.

The ultimate luxury was when I allowed Monty to share my bed. I simply did not have the heart to banish him to his crate on his last night. He clasped me tightly around the neck all night, as he snored gently into my ear. It was not the most restful night, being situated so close to the kitchen, the clamour was sustained until the early hours and our window opened onto a courtyard where the dustbins were placed, the lids of which were clanged on and off for most of the night. Any further noise Monty might have produced would have been quite drowned out by the cluttering of crockery and falsetto fantasia of one of the kitchen hands.

I awoke at 5.30am, just as the breakfast shift seemed to be starting work and the kitchen baritone came on duty. Monty was hugging and kissing me and revelling in the novelty of having a sleeping companion. He climbed out of my bed and into Doug's when he noticed him still sound asleep, but Doug pushed him away sleepily, not at all enamoured with the affectionate advances of a chimp at such an early hour.

Monty and I took our baths together, me in the conventional one and he in the bidet. I was anxious to get out of the hot, stuffy room and the smell of garbage that wafted through the window and so I took Monty for a walk to show him Las Palmas. I had not been prepared for the attention he would attract, unlike in The Gambia, it was more a matter of showing him to Las Palmas.

Early morning workers striding out mechanically on their daily route were halted in their tracks at the sight of a young chimpanzee in the company of a skinny, fair-haired foreigner. I went from bar to bar endeavouring to purchase some milk for Monty and a coffee for myself. Men slouched on bar stools, sipping lugubriously at their first Funtador of the day, stared open-mouthed, lest the simian apparition tucked under my arm be the onset of DTs! Several people were rude enough to laugh at the youngster and I was finding it increasingly difficult to restrain his punching arm.

The silver moustached manager was in the foyer when we returned to the hotel and still eyed Monty somewhat warily. He asked if we had enjoyed our stay and I told him we had and apologised for Monty's untypical outrageous behaviour of the previous afternoon and explained the flight had upset him. He smiled, warming towards us and so I asked Monty to thank the kind man for letting him stay, expecting him to merely shake hands. To the Senor's consternation, Monty flung both arms around his neck and planted one of his most squelchy kisses squarely upon his lips.

I wondered why I had worried so about Monty's booster jab, for when the time came, inevitably Doug did it, without Monty even being aware he had been injected, as I held him to me. I felt Doug might have been prompted by the distinct possibility of my hammering on the President's suite door, seeking his veterinary expertise. The bus was already waiting and we hastily collected our luggage and rushed onto it. It was only after we had boarded that we realised we had left the hypodermic syringe on the dressing table. We imagined the management concluding they had not only harboured a couple of eccentric Britons who travelled with a chimpanzee, but junkies to boot!

On the bus, Monty sat drowsily on my lap, listening to an elderly German lady sitting next to me who cooed baby-like endearments to him in her own tongue, as he gently traced the pattern of her floral dress with his forefinger. He then fell soundly asleep, the injection had obviously been effective and this time I hoped it would have a more lasting soporific effect.

Doug found me a seat and left us in the airport terminal whilst he went to check Monty in and enquire about our flight. We were to leave Monty here once we had seen him safely on his way, for he was being met at Gatwick by the zoo officials and we were going on to one of the other islands for a few days. I looked down at his small flat face, twitching in an innocent chimpanzee dreamland and wishing I could have kept him with me a little longer. My idyll was rudely disrupted when Monty flashed open his eyes and I did not like the impish expression that gleamed out of them.

He leapt off my lap and was off and away, and far from the compliant, little chimp we all knew and loved – the Jekyll and Hyde formula had struck again!

Fearlessly and totally uninhibited, Monty set about producing a trail of havoc. I had lost sight of him, but judging by the vexed expression on the young lady's face at the Iberia Airways stand, as she gathered up leaflets that were strewn all around her counter, it was apparent he had recently passed that way. I arrived in the bar just in time to see him break into a way-out dance routine, miraculously avoiding the glasses of drinks lined up along the counter. I could hardly believe it was Monty for he had all the panache of Bill Brewer himself and had obviously been impressed by him. I grabbed him and dragged him out, but he escaped my grasp and after pausing to toss out a few books from the paperback stand, he dashed into the florists. There he set about rearranging the displays of bird of paradise flowers, before ducking out of my reach again. Then to my utter horror – he bounded into the Gents toilet! Did I dare? No, I didn't. I hovered anxiously outside, as a stream of bewildered-looking gentlemen filed out. After he had apparently vacated the convenience of all occupants, I heard a series of door slamming and toilet flushing and then Monty himself came galloping out, with a stream of toilet roll trailing behind.

Continuing in an abandoned vein, he pranced around the terminal with a waggish grin spread across his face and me screaming hysterically in his wake. After tight-rope walking the backs of a row of seats, causing minor pandemonium as the occupants panicked and fled, he sauntered over to where a man was mopping the floor. Making it quite apparent he had not used the facilities whilst he was in the Gents, he stood in front of the cleaner and blatantly urinated.

Judging by the vexed expression on the young lady's face at the Iberian Airways Stand

“Gracias” the benign man nodded to him, obviously taking it to be some essential part of his toilet training and set about mopping it up.

Monty then proceeded with his frolic, leading me on a relentless chase, as I hastily apologised for each fresh disaster I encountered. Everyone was most understanding in the circumstances.

He had just pounced into an open suitcase at the Customs Desk and gathered up a handful of neckties, when I managed to grab hold of him before he had a chance to discover any contraband items.

I dragged his limp form by one arm, as he giggled and bumped along, over towards a coffee bar, hoping something to eat and drink might distract him from further pranks.

“For zees?” the bartender spat, when I endeavoured to purchase a glass of cold milk. However, a more kindly-disposed washer-up produced a receptacle capable of withstanding chimpanzee contamination and poured the milk into it. I suspected it was an ashtray and they appeared to think he would go down on all fours and lap it up like a dog or cat, and looked most surprised when he sipped it from the thick rim.

Refreshed by his drink and munching on a biscuit, Monty appeared reinvigorated and all set for another round of frolic, but I kept a firm hold. I noticed Doug at the British Caledonian counter and we went over to him.

“Where on earth have you been? I’ve been looking all over for you.”

“That’s about where we have been” I said exhaustedly, as I was beginning to feel quite limp.

The checking-in clerks had been most considerate and allowed Monty to be the last to board the plane, notwithstanding the Gambian President himself. I placed Monty in his crate and kissed him goodbye, he was well stocked with mangoes and bananas to sustain him throughout the flight.

I felt suddenly anonymous and unencumbered walking back through the scene of recent chaos. I have re-experienced the same sensation when I have since been at Las Palmas airport, almost expecting people to remember and point me out. I appreciated the anonymity of being a non-chimpanzee-carrying passenger.

“There she is, that’s the lady” a little boy had cried that day, as he pointed to me.

“Don’t be a naughty boy, you must stop telling lies” his mother scolded.

“But she did, she had a monkey, I saw it in the lavatory.”

I went up onto the observation balcony to watch Monty’s plane take off, whilst Doug checked our luggage in. I felt saddened for the hairy little chap, going away from Africa to take up his new and unfamiliar life.

“Il relativo?” an old, Spanish man standing beside me asked.

“Si.” I nodded, longing to add, “A close relative of all of us.” But my Spanish did not extend to Darwinism.

* * * * * * * *

CHAPTER 8
A GARRULOUS OLD BIRD

We had only been back in The Gambia a few hours after our leave when our next pet arrived. I found her on the back doorstep when I got up in the morning – a squirming puppy of about three weeks, the first of many to mysteriously materialise on our doorstep. Her coat was alive with fleas and she was covered in weeping sores, which must have been caused by the virulent flies that swarm in the rains and plague the dogs.

I cleaned her up and fed her, stipulating she could not possibly stay, but by that time Paddy was wearing his "what a sweet little thing" expression and Baba and Candy immediately asked the inevitable,

"Can we keep her?"

"No" I answered, "let me see, what can we call her?"

That is where I always go wrong, for once an animal had a name however young, it instantly takes on an identity that makes it impossible to reject it. As she was sable and looked rather like a lion cub, we decided upon Simba.

Even at that early age, she made it apparent that she disliked people as intensely as Paddy loved them, and apart from our immediate daily circle, she would tolerate nobody and retreated into a corner, snarling and growling if anyone strange came in.

She instantly accepted and adored Jimmy Jos though, an old African Grey parrot that sported a jazzy red tail and at that impressionable age, adopted him as her master. Jim was quite an ancient fellow and perhaps it was by virtue of his years that he commanded Simba's obedient respect.

"Simba – Come on, Simba!" he would call, if she ran out to bark at the gate. "S-i-m-b-a!" he would boom, in exasperation, if she did not immediately respond. His commands would be interspersed with dog-calling whistles, and his tone grew more testy, the longer he had to call her.

The parrot Jimmy belonged to the vet Donnie Graham and his wife, and stayed with us when they were away on leave. He was with us for a considerable time whilst Donnie was in London having medical treatment.

From the first, Paddy had totally ignored him, as if talking parrots were so commonplace in West Africa as to be beneath his contempt. Likewise, Jimmy ignored him and although he soon mastered the names of everyone in the household, he never once called him Paddy. Admittedly, as one would expect at his age, he could confuse names, particularly if he had been dozing when Simba barked and would revert to the name of his master's dog, Susie.

"Sue, Sums.... Sueba.....Simba" he would get at last.

The amazing fact was that Simba invariably obeyed him and rushed over obediently to his cage upon being summoned but in consequence never learned the same degree of compliance to our commands. The only way I was ever able to control her was by impersonating Jimmy's baritone pitch, as his voice definitely tended towards the masculine, even though his actual gender was open to conjecture. It was a little disconcerting to onlookers, when on trying to retrieve Simba I would instinctively break into a voice one would rather associate with an elderly, irascible, military gentleman. Not that she often needed retrieving, as once left in our compound she chose never to step outside again on her own four paws. So Baba had instigated her early outings by carrying her in a shopping basket, trying to cure her of her agoraphobia and this mode of conveyance had to be sustained for most of her life.

Simba had an insatiable, indiscriminate appetite, whereas Jimmy was something of a discerning eater. He would therefore toss out any groundnuts he considered unfit for avian consumption to Simba, as she begged beneath his cage. Groundnuts tended to become her staple diet and being of a similar colour, from eating so many she soon became a similar shape, until Baba despaired that she was turning into one.

The parrot also became her puppyhood playmate, as he was not averse to a game of tug-of-war with one of his chewing sticks. If anyone else had dared stick their head through his open door, he would have soon bitten it – that is with the exception of Landing, of course.

When Jimmy Jos was in residence, Landing once more came into his own.

"Down there Jimmy boy" Landing would use his lion-taming voice, and sure enough, the fastest beak on the West African coast did not so much as twitch. Landing would then unhurriedly clean out the cage, defying the bird to bite him and of course, as Landing confidently predicted, he never did.

If I dared to so much as attempt to change his water, it was more a matter of catch-as-catch-can, and usually he did! I would take out his water trough whilst he was safely sitting outside on top of his cage and he would regard me with a definite air of challenge. However quickly I ran to the kitchen, washed the tray and refilled it, by the time I returned Jimmy would be back inside sitting on his perch crooning some blandishment as he watched my dilemma.

"Hello then. Who's a clever boy?"

With his ready command of names, which he would instantly switch back to on subsequent visits, Jimmy generally had the household running around in circles for most of the day.

"Landing, Landing!" he would summon, and after a few seconds began tut-tutting impatiently, before repeating the name. He sounded like some old, Colonial resident, which of course he was, who found the servants of today singularly lacking in servility!

"Fardou" he would spit out Fatou's name the way Landing did and however frequently he called her, Fatou would always appear at once, answering in unfamiliar English,

"Yes Jimmy." As if he were about to impart some prophetic news.

We were all constantly at the mercy of Jimmy's practical jokes, as apart from speaking, anyone who has ever known an African Grey will be only too well aware of their ability to imitate sounds. How often I would go to the French Doors in response to a knocking on glass noise or to the back door to the distinctive knocking on wood. Landing always answered this assuming it must be somebody of the lowerarchy, in Jeeves-like response,

"Yerse. Come." Which naturally Jimmy soon picked up and would chorus with him.

Consequently, after a while we tended to go about our business without responding to our names being called and ignoring people knocking on the doors. He did afford me something of a

Simba! Landing! Fatou!

sociable reputation though, I must admit. When his cage was out on the veranda in the morning, he would call to people passing by.

"Coo-ee! Coo-ee!" when they would either come in to find out what I wanted or wave and call back in greeting. He also made Doug seem something of a bounder by wolf-whistling when Doug was ostensibly alone on the veranda. Particularly one day when two scantily dressed Scandinavian ladies were passing – his vocalisation was always so aptly timed.

At least he did not acquire a neighbouring parrot's habit of hooting like a car horn. The girls and I were always amused watching people leap out of the road as a loud blast indicated a car was nearly upon them. He had such a variety of horns too, from the sedately genteel limousine, a modest mini bleep to a raucous lorry blast. Although fully aware of his practice of honking, we would always react and dash to the side of the road, automatically.

My only claim to mimicry is my cockerel, and in all modesty I feel I do a pretty fair impersonation. Purely to entertain Jimmy you understand, one afternoon I gave him the benefit of my cock-crow, unaware that Landing was still in the kitchen. Landing rushed in smirking and nodding proudly in Jimmy's direction, as he took personal credit for any newly-learned party-pieces the parrot performed. I simply did not have the heart to disillusion him and I could not resist occasionally breaking out into a cock-crow. I suppose it was fortunate that Jimmy did not add this to his repertoire.

Doug seemed really thrilled the first time Jimmy moved in and unlike a chimpanzee, it appeared a parrot was something he had always rather fancied keeping. He placed him on his shoulder and chanted to Jimmy,

"Pieces of eight. Pieces of eight." Jimmy remained tacit and unimpressed but Doug did not give up, convinced that this was an essential phrase in any self-respecting parrot's vocabulary.

He decided walking around with a parrot on his shoulder was more his style – a style which was unfortunately short-lived! I saw Jimmy, beak poised, taking aim, but the blood was gushing from Doug's neck before I was able to warn him!

Then he discovered that parrots could be added to his long list of allergies and Jimmy's proximity triggered off long sneezing sessions, which Jimmy would also join in. He was well practised in the art of sneezing, which was accompanied by sniffling and nose blowing noises, imitating the worst possible cold. His owner told an amusing story of when the much-travelled bird had been aboard ship. He had been cared for by the butcher and housed adjacent to the galley. On handing back the caged bird to Donnie at Southampton the butcher appeared ill at ease.

"Is he alright?" Donnie asked

"I'm afraid I don't know how to tell you this sir, but we have all had the most shocking colds down here this trip and I'm afraid your parrot has caught it. He's been sneezing his ruddy head off!"

He was certainly a wily, old bird with a devilish sense of humour. He had a way of lulling one into a false sense of security, with his head lowered, he would 'pssss!' and cluck demurely, indicating he would like his crown to be stroked, but no sooner was finger placed on head, when it would slowly rotate, and fixing one with his beady, yellow eye – 'stab' he would have you! Was it coincidental that such assaults were followed by a demonic laugh?

His manner of telling a joke, although unintelligible, was so realistic, he would have me in stitches. The monologue would be interspersed with throaty chuckles as it built up to the inaudible but hilarious punch-line. This would be followed by his own outrageous laughter, breaking up into a nasty smoker's cough. It was as infectious as the "Laughing Policeman" song, but somehow I felt the jokes were not entirely clean. He had a wide range of laughter, from a feminine genteel titter, a smug throaty chuckle to the most raucous bellowing. I wondered who the original humorists were, from whom they had been acquired over his many years.

Being something of a yarn-spinner himself, he responded to any well-told joke or anecdote. Marion's conversations were always punctuated by Jimmy tittering in the background in a manner of those heard at ladies' coffee mornings. Unfortunately, he could not distinguish the humorous tale from the tragic with most embarrassing consequences at times.

A distressed British citizen called in one evening and told us of the long series of disasters that had plagued him, as Jimmy perched on the top of his cage listening intently.

"I lost my passport when I had the burglary and hadn't had a chance to get another, when I heard my mother had died. So I missed the funeral."

"Ha ha, ha." Jimmy chortled indicating this was really going to be a good one.

Doug and I both shot glances at him.

"I didn't really intend coming back for a second tour, not after Dorothy had left me, so I stored all my effects, then they had a flooding at the warehouse."

"Ho. Ho. Ho! He! He! Ha! Ha!" He was really building up ready for the punch-line.

The man paused to glance over his shoulder dolefully at the hilarious bird, without comment, before going on.

"I wanted to bring the children out for the holiday, but I can't get them on my passport until the custody is settled. Just as well though, I'm really camping out over there, I haven't got a thing, not even a radio."

"Ha! Ha! Ha! Eh! Eh! Splutter, wheeze, cough, snort."

"Shut up Jimmy" I said out of the corner of my mouth. "Shall we take our drinks outside, it seems a bit warm in here." I suggested tactfully.

As Jimmy's cage was situated in the corner beside the french door, which callers normally used, it sometimes proved disconcerting when I opened the door to them. On opening my mouth to speak, as I paused to draw breath, Jimmy would interject in deep baritone Jeeves-like tone,

"Yerse?"

Leaving me standing with my mouth wide open like a ventriloquist's dummy and the caller truly amazed.

"It was the *jobo*." I would explain, pointing out Jimmy.

Jimmy quickly took advantage of anyone strange and unfamiliar with his lethal beak. If a newcomer was working around the house, however I warned them, they paid no heed. I would hear the inevitable slashing sound of ripped cloth followed by a surprised cry and knew they had passed too close to the cage.

He appeared so innocuous to anyone that did not know him, chatting in a friendly voice, luring them near but I recognised the quivering anticipation and the gleam in his rigidly fixed eye, as it focused on an approaching expanse of flesh.

I had made little progress with the *Mandinka* language but as Jimmy incantated the long greeting frequently, I soon picked it up.

"Salaam Alekum"	-	Peace be with you.
"Alekum Salaam"	-	With you be peace.
"Hera be?"	-	Are you at peace?
"Hera darang"	-	Peace only
"Sumo'le?"	-	How are the people of your compound?
"I be je"	-	They are there
"Kortana nte?"	-	I hope there is no trouble
"Tana nte"	-	There is no trouble at all

Thanks to Jimmy teaching me parrot-fashion, I was then able to greet and respond to everyone I met, although I did find it somewhat hampered my progress in a crowded market. Despite Jimmy's reciting the *Wolof* equivalent just as frequently, I somehow never got further than,

"Kerabe"

"Keradrong"

Similarly when he said "Pardon?" or "*Ikoo?*" in *Mandinka*, I would find myself automatically repeating what I had said simply for the benefit of a parrot.

Our choice of music tended to be to Jimmy's taste, Judy Garland being his favourite and 'Over the Rainbow' especially. He would squawk throughout a Sinatra record, nor was he too keen on Nat King Cole.

"Some, some" he would shout, skipping to 'bow'. We invariably gave in, of course. It then became a nightly ritual that Doug would sing it to him and he would not retire without his lullaby. When I attempted to sing it to him, I fear I got the same reaction as Sinatra and felt like a third rate chanteuse in a sleazy club.

"Get her off."

He was quite a linguist was Jim. A Nigerian visitor was delighted to discover he knew something of her dialect and after some French visitors had left, I was not surprised to hear him reeling off a few French phrases, with an impeccable accent, of course.

Christmas in The Gambia is celebrated vigorously, even though it is a predominantly Moslem country. The clamour gets underway early on Christmas morning, when continuous groups of boys, clad in leaves, called *Kangkarangs* visit all the compounds banging loudly on tin cans, dancing and shouting. The object seems to be to make as much noise as possible. Every boy in the province appears to pursue this aspect of the festive season most persistently, as I am sure the belief prevails that when the *tubabolus* are so full of Christmas goodwill, they will tolerate anything and be most generous. It was possible to feel quite benevolent to the first batch of young Christmas visitors and I suspect this might have been a mistake, as word soon passed around and some young hopefuls would continue to call well into the New Year, until the vegetation that adorned them withered and shed, leaving the garden appearing most autumnal.

By New Years' Day it seemed that every inhabitant of Bakau, if not several other villages, had visited us more than once and this could not have been better, as far as Jimmy Jos was concerned. He would continue to emulate the deep male voices and soprano trills through to mid-January, going into a noticeable decline towards the end of the month when he realised that the festive visitors had stopped calling. For that matter, so did the local inhabitants, everyone drooping exhaustedly inert, as if reserving their energies for the next scheduled jamboree.

I had been offered an African Grey parrot on arrival in The Gambia but had unhesitatingly declined. I had always considered the keeping of birds in bondage for one's amusement, whilst they recited inane sounds and phrases, as one of the cruellest aspects of bird-kind. However, having lived with Jimmy Jos it was difficult to concede that he was at all unhappy, apart from the occasional afternoon boredom when he would resort to hacking at the curtains or pecking his way through his perch. Jimmy certainly appeared to make the most of his captive life and had forgotten his wild, avian behaviour except for when it rained. At the first clap of thunder and pitter-patter on the roof that indicated the rains had arrived, Jimmy would step into his drinking trough and proceed to bathe. It was the only time he did it and only then was there a reminder of the free-flying bird which he must once have been. Or when he listened to ‘Over the Rainbow’ with avid concentration, I fancied I glimpsed a tear running down his beak at the line ‘Birds fly over the rainbow, why then oh why can’t I?’

* * * * * * * *

CHAPTER 9
ROCK-A-BYE CHIMPY

In March there was a virulent outbreak of canine distemper to which Paddy had succumbed without our knowledge. Simba too had come down with it but I had taken her to the vet for immediate treatment. Unfortunately, it coincided with one of Paddy's longer absences away from home. By the time he did return, he was staggering, his breathing was laborious and despite the treatment he received, he died on the second day.

So it was that Paddy never met Flint and I knew he would have loved him. Simba's reaction to the hairy apparition on introduction was paralysed horror, causing her to urinate on the spot.

I had not known of the arrival of another young chimpanzee in *Abuko* until I went out for a visit and saw one on the back of one of the wardens. The man was endeavouring to erect fences with the baby chimp clinging to his back tenaciously. My heart gave a lurch at the sight of him, I had so missed Titan and life had never seemed quite the same without a chimp around the house. A surge of broodiness rose up from my stomach, chest to throat, until I could hardly speak.

"Where has the *ndemo* come from?" I asked.

"Dis small boy *ndemo* the Police take from one man who bring him to The Gambia."

I stroked the infant's silky skinned face as he looked up at me dolefully pouting, tightening his grip more determinedly on the man's shirt. His head appeared over-large for his tiny body, and his small compact face was fanned with sparse black hair. He looked like an adorable, living rag doll.

"Can I hold him?" I asked and the man appeared only too pleased to relinquish him. For as fond as he was of the chimps, he did not really see himself in the role of foster-mother it was clear to see.

He appeared weightless in my arms and he pressed his soft face to snuggle under my chin.

I went in search of Eddie, holding on tightly to the precious baby ape.

Flint appeared weightless

I found Eddie Brewer and his daughter Heather and they were busy slapping green paint on the newly-erected 'Tarzans' and 'Janes' *Abuko*-styled conveniences.

"Hello Jan. I see you find him den, I dink you might!" He and Heather exchanged amused glances. "One of the bagmen was lugging him around, the blighter, as if he doesn't make enough money out of wildlife from his skin bags. The little chap seems in good condition though, don't you think?"

"Yes, he seems fine. Perfect in fact." I agreed as I gazed at the exquisite young chimp. "Er. Em. Er….. What were you going to do with him?" I at last ventured to ask.

Eddie winked at Heather and they both stood grinning at me.

"Now, let me see…" Eddie started to say thoughtfully. "What do you think Heather?"

"I think we need to find somebody who would be willing to look after him until he is a little older."

"That is an excellent idea." Eddie said. "But who?"

"I don't really know Dad. It would have to be somebody prepared to give him a lot of attention as they would have to give most of their time to him."

"I could. I would." I kept trying to butt in.

"He would need a lot of feeding up, plenty of milk."

"Yes, but I would." I tried to interrupt.

"Love and reassurance too" Heather said. "His mother would have kept him with her continuously; a young chimp needs a sense of security."

"What a pity we don't know somebody suitable" Eddie said smiling at Heather.

"Could I really keep him?" This time it was me using Baba and Candy's standard phrase.

"I say, would you really?" Eddie asked, feigning surprise. "That really is most uncommonly kind of you to offer."

By that time, the small chimp was clinging to me so possessively, I doubt that I could have parted with him, even if I had wanted to.

"Doug won't mind will he?" Eddie asked as I was leaving.

“Oh no, of course not.” I said confidently, suddenly wondering what his reactions might be to another chimp, particularly after Titan.

”What are you going to call him?” Heather asked. We mused over a few suggestions, coming to a short-list of ‘Cuddly’ and ‘Flint’ and as I tried ineffectively to get my lighter to work and commented I needed a new flint, Heather said

“I think you’ve got one, Jan.” It had also been the name of the super-sleuth we had seen at the cinema the previous evening and that appeared to settle it.

Heather was shortly leaving to start her equestrian career and her sister Stella was already away at Woburn, where she was working with elephants. At that time there were five chimps housed in the Brewer’s garden cage and they had been working hard in building a spacious enclosure for them in *Abuko.* Several antelopes had already been released into the reserve and a section fenced off for them and the first trickle of tourists beginning to visit. Funds were practically non-existent and the growing menagerie supported mainly by the Brewers themselves, so help was always being sought. The passengers from a German cruise ship, which regularly docked for a day in The Gambia now made a scheduled tour of *Abuko* and a small entrance fee was to be charged. Stella and Heather had always spent the day prior to the ship’s arrival squeezing out the juice from piles of limes to sell drinks to the visitors, in another effort to raise funds.

I doubt that a happier person had ever left *Abuko* as I went on my way, taking Flint with me. I stopped the car several times for people to admire him and I glowed with all the pride of a newly-delivered mother.

Landing did not appear very interested or surprised, merely nodding, dismissing Flint, before asking:

“What you want for *chop* tonight? You no tell me dis morning.” He admonished.

Doug appeared reasonably interested, although not wildly enthusiastic, once I reassured him that he would be no trouble whatsoever and I hastened to show him how small and ineffectual his teeth were.

Jimmy Jos started meowing and calling "Puss, puss, puss" and fully seemed to think I had brought home a cat. Having recovered from her initial shock, Simba sat squinting from beneath Doug's chair and growling from time to time.

"Oh dee *piccan*, ooh-da-boo-da-boo." Fatou went into raptures and tried to take him from me, but Flint maintained a leech-like grip. It seemed it took another woman to fully appreciate his charms.

I made the pastry, went out for a walk, ate my supper and settled down to read and Flint had not let go of me once, except when I held him out to wee.

"Where is he going to sleep?" Doug asked as the evening wore on. I had been expecting and dreading the question.

"Oh, don't worry, he will be alright with me." I chanced.

"He can't sleep with you and you don't approve of chimps wearing nappies. I thought you were going to rear him naturally so that he will settle into *Abuko* later. You don't want him to end up having to go to a zoo."

"I know" I agreed reluctantly, "But I don't fancy making a nest out in a tree in the garden and he must miss his mother. Just for tonight."

He reminded me of the number of times I had said that about new puppies and our first dog had spent the remainder of his long life trying to get into bed with us.

I hardly felt able to shove him out into Titan's cage, alone out in the night, apart from which, since Titan's noisy residence, chimp tolerance in the area was practically nil. So we finally agreed upon the small cloakroom loo.

We made a bed up for him in a cardboard carton, which bore the appropriate inscription, 'Feeds royal babies' and placed it in his new bedroom but getting him away from me and into bed was another matter. He screamed and took a firmer hold if I so much as prised a finger off until it appeared he might well become a permanent appendage.

"What's the trouble?" Landing asked as he came through with his pump to spray the bedrooms.

"We're trying to get Flint to bed. Oh, I don't think you had better use your pump now, it might *humbug* Flint."

"Hey, Her, Hoop!" Landing shouted, yanking Flint from off my back before I knew what had happened. He placed him in the carton firmly and closed the door.

His agonising screams were more than I could bear, for he was so small and helpless and needed so much reassurance at that vulnerable age. I rushed into the kitchen holding my hands over my ears, and reached for the cooking sherry to fortify myself. It was no use, I could bear it no longer, I must take him out but by the time I returned to listen outside his door, to my amazement, all was quiet.

"He's choked." I panicked.

"No he hasn't, he's alright." Doug reassured.

"He's suffocated. Is there enough air in there, you did open the window a fraction, didn't you?"

"What about the mosquitoes?" Landing asked. "Make I use my pump small bit?"

"No. No thank you, don't bother." Just the thought of those lethal fumes wafting under Flint's door, I would never sleep for worrying about him. As it was I was also cautioning him as to his liberal use on Jimmy Jos' behalf.

"I wonder if we could fit a panel of one-way glass in the toilet." I asked Doug, as I was longing to see what Flint was doing but did not dare risk disturbing him.

"I doubt the Landlord would agree to that, anyway, it could be embarrassing when it reverts to normal use again, Flint won't be here forever."

Jimmy Jos, who had been unaccustomedly quiet began to screech – he had added a new and raucous impersonation to his repertoire, young chimpanzee crying!

I was awake at first light the following morning, anxious to find out how my infant was. I had slept very little and when I did it was only to dream of baby chimps drowning in lavatories. I had got up several times during the night to creep up outside the toilet door, straining to hear the sound of his breathing, but the noise of cockroaches clanking around was all I heard. Jimmy Jos had startled me by giving a loud cough from beneath his covered cage, having heard me around.

When I opened the door, Flint was curled up and still soundly asleep, but lifted up his arms towards me as soon as he opened his eyes. He suctioned himself onto me and that was how he remained for the rest of the day. Bathing and dressing had been a little tricky, a complexity which a chimpanzee mother would not encounter. It was a lengthy procedure but I soon developed a knack of dressing and undressing, moving him from one hip to the other and bathing with him practically sitting on my head. Flint naturally found the experience very alarming and often I would no sooner have dressed, when he would wet my dress, necessitating me to repeat the process all over again.

Thus began a phase of obsessional motherhood and I came to understand why it was that ladies of erstwhile varied interest, suddenly became downright bores consumed only with their blessed and remarkable progeny. For eight months I joined the ranks of cooing, besotted babblers, constantly concerned only with my diddums chimp! I yearned to join a mother and baby circle, but there were no chimpanzee groups around! I was so tempted to contribute to discussions comparing childrens' development or concern over little Johnny's chest, but soon discovered it prudent to remain quiet. Eyebrows would shoot sky-high should I so much as comment, 'That's strange, my Flint was doing that at the same age.' Mothers do not tend to welcome hearing their unique child compared to a chimpanzee!

"Guess what he did today dear?" would be my first words when Doug walked in through the door.

Marion brought the girls in to see the new arrival and produced the ideal solution for his night-time comfort in the shape of a rag-doll. This worked like a charm, as Landing was able to relinquish his grip from me to fasten it onto the doll. He became very attached to it, much as a child does to a teddy bear, only he adopted a human comforter, rather than an animal one.

As dusk neared, Flint would become agitated, he was obviously tired and his eyelids droopy as he tried to stifle yawns. His bedtime had to be at eight o'clock precisely, and there was to be no varying of the time. Five minutes too early or late and he would struggle to stay with me and cry considerably from within the confines of his small room. By that time of evening, I appreciated being unburdened, as in the sticky climate, it was rather like carrying around a hot water bottle all day.

Although he appeared no more ambulant than a baby of similar age, he proved to be far more agile. We always left the toilet window latched on the first notch, feeling there was no danger of him trying to escape. However, when one night we sat outside talking with Marion and the girls, whilst Flint still screamed his protest in the adjacent room, I was perplexed as his cries suddenly appeared louder and more urgent. I discovered he had tumbled out of the window, but fortunately landed in a soft flower bed beneath and we realised we would have to tie the latch down.

It took a few days before Simba began to accept Flint, but when she did she was so maternal, it was difficult to dissuade her from clearing up Flint's excreta. It was due to Simba that he was persuaded to take his first faltering steps away from me. He was beginning to climb down to straddle my legs to enjoy a rocking horse game, which gave Simba an opportunity to fuss over him. She would lick his ears and nibble his neck, causing him to chuckle and push her away with one hand, until he found the courage to plonk onto the floor beside her for a game. From this he progressed to scrambling around the coffee table with Simba chasing him and so long as I remained seated, he felt quite secure. Should I so much as attempt to get to my feet though, he would instantly begin to cry and cling to my legs.

Poor Jimmy, not only had he been usurped as top attraction, he also had to share his friend Simba. I fear in those first weeks he chewed his way through quite a few perches and we had the carpenter supply several spares. I would come in and my attention be drawn towards him by one of his inane remarks, to find him standing forlornly on the bottom of his cage and his perch beside him in two halves.

He promptly put a stop to any overtures Flint made towards him and if the young chimp dared so much as peer into his cage, the scurrilous old bird would terrify him with one of his ferocious squawks. Even when he did attempt to call his name, he spat it so vehemently as to be unintelligible and hardly an invitation.

It was only when Flint was banished for the night that Jimmy really came into his own. He would commence his recital with a few deprecating chimp squeals, before leading into his non-stop chatter.

"Hello. Hello. What's the matter? Sumoli. (the Madinka greeting) Pardon?" Should he get no response he would lapse into one of his infuriatingly monotonous phrases.

"Two, two..... Two two......." Which was the first two digits of a phone number once memorised. So we would comply with Jimmy's Desert Island Discs' choice simply to shut him up.

My walks along the beach were now taken with Flint clinging to my back and Simba sitting in the shopping basket. If I sat down whilst out, Flint would clamber into the basket and cuddle up to Simba and that was about as exciting as the outings were. Ebrima still stalked us, naturally enough, and he too must have found it quite tame compared to our excursions into the interior with Titan.

Baba now came in each afternoon as soon as she was home from school to play with Flint and he found her an ideal playmate. Candy had remained wary for many weeks, but finding her sister had not sustained injury, she too began to drift in again. This was ideal for him, as he experienced the type of relationship he would have had with older brothers and sisters in a chimpanzee group. Baba had the ability to instigate games that he readily responded to and he would potter around with her, just so long as I remained in sight. I was still not able to get up and leave the room without him running after me panic-stricken. I realised this was the essential difference between him and human toddlers. It appeared unnatural to me when I heard mothers calling their farewells and leaving young children in the care of a nanny, without an histrionic outburst from the youngster.

A change of appearance also had the most petrifying effect upon Flint. When Baba arrived one afternoon adorned in an outlandish assortment of dressing-up clothes and make-up, Flint screamed inconsolably. He was terrified at the ghoulish apparition and she had gone to such lengths only to amuse him. Similarly, when one morning Doug went in to collect him and wake him up, wearing a new pair of pyjamas, we were quite unable to convince him it was really Doug. I had to patch up his old ones for him to continue wearing, lest he frighten my diddums again!

Flint did not bound into the joyous state of wakefulness that Titan had, anticipating a hearty breakfast and cups of tea. Flint sat on my lap whilst I ate breakfast, still bleary-eyed and staring dazedly and I was fortunate if I could persuade him to nibble a dunked rusk. There was no food he appeared to relish, whatever we tried, which proved a great cause for concern. Whilst we all sat yum-yumming on endless bananas to tempt him, he would barely take a perfunctory bite until even Baba was beginning to get tired of them and it was years before I could again face eating a banana. Not so Simba, who tended to identify with her pets to the extent of sharing their food. If she did not already eat enough of Jimmy's groundnuts, bananas were added to her staple diet.

When entertaining some official visitors one evening, I deemed it wise not to mention Flint's presence. He was already in bed when they arrived for a late supper and I placed a pair of step ladders and a bicycle against his room door. Even if the hallway did look a little cluttered, it would prevent anyone from blundering into the loo; if they had, I would not like to guess who would have been the more surprised, them or Flint! Unfortunately, I did not have a chance to let local guests in on the idea and had to change the subject when they asked after Flint. I was out in the kitchen trying to find out what had happened to the meal when I heard someone ask where the toilet was and dashed in on hearing them directed,

"Just outside the door on the left."

"No, no, that one is out of order." I physically yanked the man away, as he was just about to move the bike. Obviously aroused, a distinct chimpanzee whimper drifted through the door and I wondered whether I should confess all.

"What was that?" the man asked.

"Oh that, oh. Just the plumbing, it makes some funny noises, now there is a bathroom just at the end of the hallway."

I waited outside Flint's door, but he quietened down and had probably only been dreaming.

It was an interminably long and nerve-wracking evening and when Jimmy began entertaining, the proceedings became quite rowdy. I spoke in a hoarse whisper, hoping it might induce everyone to follow suit, but someone merely asked what was wrong with my throat. Jimmy was really on good form and everyone appeared reluctant to leave. Flint had started to whimper again a couple of times and somebody caught me whispering through the closed door to comfort him, when I pretended I had dropped something. I managed to direct the conversation onto our local wildlife, pointing out how noisy the owls and bats were every night, our compound being infested with nocturnal creatures. I hoped this might help to explain any strange noises they might have heard.

By the time they were leaving, the visitors had began to view me somewhat quizzically, and the cries emerging from the little room left me with no doubts that Flint was awake.

"You don't keep turkeys, do you?" One man asked as he left.

What an extraordinary thing to have said!

* * * * * * * *

CHAPTER 10
A GROWING CHIMP

I endeavoured to keep Flint out of doors as much as possible, communicating to him in the vocabulary I had learned from Titan. The stunted mangroves were excellent practise trees for him to dangle from and I demonstrated how chimpanzees made their nests. We passed trees daily that still had remnants of Titan's old nests, even after two rainy seasons. I showed him my inept termite fishing, which he soon excelled me at and pointed out edible fruits making chimp-feeding grunts. What with behaving much as Titan had, apart from the tantrums, and eating up all of Flint's unwanted bananas, I all but became a chimpanzee myself! I reached a stage where if anyone appeared in danger, I would instinctively emit a primeval hoot of alarm, rather than shout 'look out'. At tree climbing I fear I had to draw the line, for I tend to get vertigo if I so much as stand on a chair and unfortunately I may have conveyed this to Flint. Baba and Candy proved more suitable tree companions and introduced Flint to a more lofty existence, but always had to carry him down again.

Flint continued to be a finicky eater and I marvelled that he continued to thrive and grow. He did fall victim to a couple of nasty fevers giving me cause for anxiety, but chimps seemed outside the veterinary range and whilst more analogous to childish ails, I could hardly take him to our local GP. I relied instead on junior asprin and a dosing of *jumbukaturri.* An old lady in the market had introduced me to it, on noticing Flint's languor one day. It was the local elixir from strange infusions, the ingredients of which I would not care to conject but the results were spectacular.

People also pressed *ju-jus* upon him to ward off evils that children are particularly prone to and everything seemed worth ensuring his well-being. These were little filled leather pouches to be worn around the neck or waist. They were always placed on babies at birth and most of the older Gambians wore some fetish, although not as many as Pa Sangyang, who was weighed down with them. The most intriguing that I came across was a young man wearing what I realised was an intra-uterine device, dangling like a pendant around his neck. I hesitated to speculate how he had come by it and whether he wore it to ward off unwanted pregnancies!

Flint spent most of his day playing in a large unused bird-cage out on the veranda, where he kept his weird assortment of possessions. He would potter in and out, as long as I was sitting nearby and often go inside and shut the door. It seemed ironical that a chimp who was not to experience the confines of a cage should choose to shut himself in one. He always took his rag doll in with him, which he dragged around everywhere and many was the panic at bedtime as we rushed around searching for it, as putting him to bed was impossible without his rag doll.

I fear he soon imposed upon Simba's good naturedness and treated her much the same as his rag doll if I did not stop him. He pulled at her paws and turned her over by her legs and she was extremely tolerant and never snapped at him. He was constantly fascinated by her teeth as he levered up her flabby lip and poked at her incisors and canines. I later found him testing his own immature teeth on her paw and when I reprimanded him, he poked the back of his hand into Simba's mouth, as if inviting her to bite it.

I was relieved to discover that his reaction to a snake (albeit a dead one) was fear. We were having lunch at the time with a newcomer to Africa, when Landing came into the dining room triumphantly.

"Lookum, bad snake dis one." A large puff adder corpse was suddenly dangled over the table.

"We find it in the garage, go kill it."

Flint leapt off the chair next to me and onto my lap and our horrified lady visitor, all but did likewise! Just as we had gone to such lengths to reassure her that predatory snakes did not lurk in every corner seeking a victim.

I tried to change the subject but she could hardly fail to hear Landing rambling on in the kitchen,

"Kill it. Er Eh! Kill it!" and Jimmy in mocking feminine squeals, screeching and tittering. She declined the sweet when Landing brought it in!

After about three months, Flint seemed sufficiently independent of me to be left with KJ, the Soccer Star Captain, later PC 443 and then Superintendent, who was a willing babysitter. I did not find it easy to walk out with Flint's deprecating screams still ringing in my ears, but KJ assured me he quietened once I was out of sight. He would play with him until eight, when he told me, without my being around, Flint would compliantly take himself off to bed.

Although Flint did not pose the same problems that Titan had, I soon discovered what hazards a house contains for an inquisitive, young chimpanzee. My attention had not been distracted for more than a minute from Flint, as I made a cup of coffee in the kitchen one day, when he was at risk. He had opened a bottom cupboard, extracted a tin and swigged the contents.

"What was in it?" I called to Landing as I snatched the tin away from him.

"Dee medicine for my pump" he replied, confirming my worse fears that it was *DDT*.

Sensing my agitation, Flint started to scream. I forced my fingers down his throat, vaguely recalling hearing that chimps do not vomit but he at least heaved up some of the lethal smelling liquid.

He became drowsy and limp and still reeked of *DDT*. I rang the doctor's surgery and they suggested large quantities of cold tea. I threw in some liver salts and *jumbukaturri* for good measure but Landing restrained me as I was about to also add a few worming tablets. Forcing large quantities of the effervescent beverage down the throat of a semi-conscious chimp who normally took no more than a perfunctory sip of a drink, was not an easy task.

Throughout the anxious day, as Flint remained drowsy, my mind raced with a rehearsed explanation if I should have to tell the Brewers the worst. I tried to keep him awake and get him on his feet, but was not too sure whether this only applied to horses suffering from colic, but everything seemed worth a try.

He then developed such violent diarrhoea that I began to wonder whether the cure had not been more detrimental than the poison. I thought it was as well I had not also administered the worming tablets.

He remained lethargic throughout the following day, but it at least appeared he was going to survive.

I admonished Landing on the folly of leaving poisons within reach, not only of Flint but his own children too. I was aware that now Flint was more mobile, he would have to be constantly watched.

Alert as I thought I was, it only takes a couple of seconds for a young chimpanzee to come to grief, in fact, just the time it took me to take a mouthful of soup before glancing back to Flint again. In that time, he had climbed the standard lamp and before I rushed over to him, he had already let out the most anguishing scream.

There was no bulb in the socket and as Flint had ascended the stand, he must have switched the lamp on. I realised with horror that the burning smell I became aware of was scorched flesh. The skin around the nail of Flint's forefinger had been practically burnt away and unlike Titan, he was the most unco-operative patient. He would not let me dress it and soon took off any bandage I attempted to put on. Marion brought along some antiseptic powder from her inexhaustible medicine chest and we were at least able to sprinkle some onto the burnt finger, provided we distracted his attention.

Flint walked around with his forefinger poised for some time and would hold it up to anyone he met. From this he progressed to a more impertinent gesticulation.

He was at a stage of experimenting with facial expressions before the dressing table mirror. He discovered a most hideous effect could be achieved by curling up his upper lip to almost cover his nose. In the process of this particular grimace he found he could produce a rather spectacular noise. Forsaking all natural chimpanzee vocalisation, he began to spend his days letting forth a series of juicy raspberries. How was Jimmy to resist so splendid a sound and he naturally mimicked Flint! Between them they maintained a positive barrage of fruity-tooties!

"Dis bad. African people no like it." Landing complained.

"Europeans aren't too keen either" I told him but try as we did, there was no dissuading Flint from blowing the offensive sound. This, combined with his jutting finger, prompted some cheeky village lads to signal back with a 'V' sign. He only had to see it the once and readily adopted this too. The doubly derisive gesticulations gave him the appearance of something of an impudent urchin. There was little I could do about the raspberries but I was at least able to hold down his protrusile fingers, much as I had had to restrain Monty's punching arm.

Flint enjoyed meeting the tradespeople that called, although he did not actively participate in the purchasing as Titan had, the

The doubly derisive gesticulations gave him the appearance of something of an impudent urchin

men tended to attribute the same astuteness to the young chimp. I fear their respect towards him somewhat waned when he began running out to them, performing his insulting greeting.

It was some months before the curio-seller who had originally brought Flint into the country for sale, called upon us. Flint reacted to the man on sight, even reverting to a more conventional chimpanzee greeting in his surprise.

Laming, the bagman, seemed quite pleased to see him, even though he had been confiscated from him, and asked if Mr Brewer had given him to me. Although I denied it, from the way Flint clambered onto the man, he was obviously familiar to him. Laming made a great fuss of him and from Flint's effusive reactions, it was apparent that he had not suffered in the man's care. Holding no grudge, Laming commented how pleased he was that I had Flint and how happy I must be. I tried to explain that I should have been happier knowing Flint could have stayed in the bush with his own family. He was a widely travelled man and told me of the wild chimpanzee groups he had seen. I was fascinated to hear his observations of them, as I had never met anyone before who had encountered them in the wild. I endeavoured to persuade him that in view of their depleting numbers, they should remain in the natural state he had seen them but he insisted that people had to shoot them when they raided their crops and infants were only 'rescued' when orphaned. It seemed that however enlightened people in Europe became regarding wildlife conservation, any efforts they make are futile whilst attitudes do not change at the remote African source.

On Sunday mornings at first demur – or flush of cistern - from within the little room (as he occasionally used the facilities), I would rise and collect Flint. I usually took him with me into the spare room, where he would potter around whilst I bathed and dressed in the adjoining bathroom. He usually sat on the edge of the bath, dangling his feet in, or lathering his hands and was never out of sight. One Sunday, after a particularly late night, I did the inadmissible, flopping onto the spare bed and fell into a sound sleep. I should have been warned, as I had a vague recollection of being subjected to the eye-lid lifting test, that chimps tend to carry out to ensure someone is really sleeping, much as toddlers do.

I doubt that I could have dozed for more than half an hour but when I did open my eyes, I blinked several times, wondering what could possibly have hit the room. It had all the appearance of having been thoroughly ransacked by a skilled burglar and there was hardly anything left in the cupboards or drawers, whilst the floor was littered with the contents.

Amidst this devastation sat Flint, wearing a pair of red panties cave-man fashion, across one shoulder and leg, over which hung a bra, slung over his head and his face was liberally embellished with lipstick and eyeshadow, with toothpaste smeared around his mouth. An eyebrow pencil protruded from his mouth and he was busy brushing his hair. I traced the heady aroma which permeated the room to a mixture of the opened bottles of perfume and a discarded smelling salts. In the bathroom, towels had been plunged into the toilet, toothpaste trails wormed over the side of the bath and talcum powder dusted over the floor.

Once I was sure that no harm had befallen him, I could hardly fail to be amused visualising the glorious exploration he had obviously thoroughly enjoyed. How often he must have watched me as I dressed and put make-up on my face, longing to use it himself. How long he must have coveted all those tempting accoutrements. In a way I was sorry I had never let him dress up, as he always displayed a proclivity for clothing and I am sure would have loved a wardrobe of his own.

Everyone that has ever kept a chimpanzee in a house, seems to have one of these ransacking incidents at some time, but it is never allowed to happen more than once.

He had been with us for eight months and during that time had grown from a helpless, bewildered infant to an inquisitive, adventurous chimpanzee. The sleeping box, which he had originally wallowed in, he now overlapped. The dog who had towered over him gigantically, he now dwarfed and the humans he had been so reliant upon, he was now indifferent to. He was becoming quite bold and adventurous and would often climb out of the window up onto an overhanging ledge, heedless if we should call him down. He would sit up there with his chin thrust out self-reliantly in a pose which was becoming part of his character. He would totter out into the garden alone and play, contentedly climbing up and down the step ladder and leaping from the top rung.

Flint ransacked the room

I speculated that the time was rapidly approaching when he would wander further afield to Titan's former favourite haunts.

It became more evident daily that he was ready to take up his place in chimpanzee society and leave behind the paraphernalia of domesticity.

I had only two reservations, firstly his inability to descend from a tree once he had recklessly clambered up to the top of it, and his intolerance to rain.

The wardens in *Abuko* had thought it hilarious when, whilst on a visit there, he had ascended into the lofty boughs of a tree, only to scream in terrified panic on finding himself up so high. I had to ask one of the men if he would kindly go up and rescue him and I felt a chimp suffering from vertigo could be a handicap in a natural, arboreal life.

Similarly with rain, should we be caught out in a downpour, Flint turned into a writhing, screeching maniac unless I sheltered him with an umbrella. As the chimps in *Abuko* were hardly likely to carry brollies around, I wondered how he would cope in the tropical deluges he would be exposed to.

* * * * * * * *

CHAPTER 11
A BUNCH OF APES

I had taken Flint out to *Abuko* quite frequently so as to keep him in touch with his simian friends. Three of the chimps now lived in the spacious enclosure which encompassed a couple of trees and was equipped with tree houses, hammocks, ropes and other diversions. Stella had returned from England and spent her mornings out walking around the reserve with the chimps. She was encouraging them to search for and forage on the abundance of natural food there was in *Abuko* and was beginning to regard our original dream of rehabilitating them to the wild as a distinct possibility.

The newly installed chimps, William and Annie, were three or four years old and Cheetah a little older. At first, Flint found the trio somewhat overpowering and it was almost as if he had no memory of his own species. However, when Annie made a friendly overture towards him, he responded with an embrace which cemented their future close relationship. Annie was something of a loner and had only ever attached herself to Heather. Once Heather, Stella's younger sister left, she showed no sign of transferring that affection to anyone else, until she took Flint under her wing.

I also took him to visit the younger chimps in the Brewer's compound, where he befriended Happy. Happy was nearer to his own age and once their initial shyness of each other was overcome, they began to romp and play together. They tickled and leapt, frolicking around until they were breathless with guileless chimpanzee laughter. So engrossed was he in his games with Happy, Flint became quite indifferent to my presence. To the extent that I was able to walk out of the compound and get into and start the car without him attempting to follow. This was the ultimate proof that he was ready to leave us and I could confidently return him to the company of other chimpanzees.

The day I had arranged to take him back *Abuko* could not have been worse as far as the weather was concerned. I had waited throughout the morning for the torrential downpour to ease but it showed no signs of abating when I took him out there in the afternoon. The chimps had been joined by another youngster, Pooh, and the four of them were huddled together in their tree house. They peered out at us inquisitively as we arrived and when I saw them my heart sank – they all had streaming colds.

Flint was already protesting vehemently at the teaming rain and when I put him down and walked away, his screams rose to an anguished pitch. I watched as he attempted to climb the ladder to join the others, but they hooted down at him, flailing their arms as if shooing him away. Flint sat piteously at the foot of the ladder with the rain glistening on his black hair and trickling down his face like teardrops, clutching pathetically to his rag doll.

My problem was that I had projected this scene in my mind so often, the symbolical gesture of handing back one chimpanzee to his rightful habitat. The others would have rushed over to welcome him and after a friendly acrobatic romp, they would have walked off, arms around each other, into the sunset, stepping forth into an idyllic future. Flint would have been unaware of my leaving and I could have gone away with the sound of chimpanzee laughter ringing in my ears, confident that he no longer needed me.

Instead of which I tore myself away reluctantly, conscious of Flint's implacable screams, rejected by his new companions and abandoned in a tropical storm. I realised I was reacting like an over-protective mother, leaving her child in the playground on the first day of school, exposed to the elements and bullies.

Only with the greatest difficulty did I manage to stay away from *Abuko* for the first few weeks of Flint's reinstallation. The time passed so slowly and I was constantly badgering the Brewers for news of him.

"How is he?" I would ask Eddie without preamble.

"Who us, yes thank you we be fine, how you keep?" he would obtusely reply.

At last I would find out that Flint and the other chimps were all well, but still I wondered whether they might not be keeping some dreadful news from me. He most certainly would have caught the others' colds as he had never had one before, which could so easily have turned into pneumonia or worse – what if he had been killed by a hyena, taking it to be a dog! He might well have fallen out of a tree, without anyone around to bring him down, or even escaped and at that very moment trying to make his way home to me. All sorts of improbable mishaps constantly niggled me.

"Daw I come beg one cigarette modom" Jimmy chanted, having taken up Ebrima the village lad's catch phrase in the same fatuous tones.

"Tickle, tickle tickle" he called and a large, black puppy bounded up to his cage (having been named Tickle because he responded to one of Jimmy's more facetious party pieces, and the only name he would subsequently answer to). He was the latest puppy to have been left on our doorstep and his oversized paws indicated he would grow large and be too expensive for a local family to keep and so he had also moved in.

"Ha ha!" Landing had come in on the morning of his arrival, rubbing his hands as if he had caught the Yorkshire Ripper red-handed.

"Dis Bear, he be the one."

Bear was an ancient dog of Chow-like appearance who belonged to some neighbours and was looked after by the Foons when they were away. He spent most of his day patrolling between the two houses and so we saw him quite frequently.

"What had Bear done?" I asked, feeling it nothing more extraordinary than raiding the dustbin.

"He the one bring the *piccans*."

We had always taken the benefactor who bestowed us with puppies as being some animal-loving local person. It did explain why we had never seen anyone at the time.

After Flint had been back in *Abuko* for several weeks, Stella assured me it was quite alright to visit him as there was no danger of unsettling him. Naturally I doubted this, convinced he would still be pining for me and just waiting for the day when we would be reunited.

As we wound our way around the paths through the lush vegetation, the air was vibrant with birdsong and it was good to be back in *Abuko*. Monkeys chattered and crashed through the tree-tops overhead. Whilst still well out of sight of the chimp enclosure, shrill, shrieking calls started up in the distance and the chimps were obviously aware of our approach.

As we neared, the rasping, grunting chorus built up into a crescendo of excited, screeching welcome. It was such a thrilling sound to hear their uninhibited cries within a natural environment, having had to quell the volume of such exuberance within the confines of suburbia. The chimps were dotted along the chain link fencing and I was not at first able to distinguish Flint, until amidst the welcoming hoots I picked out an intermittent raspberry!

"Flint!" I cried, holding out my arms. "My little Flint, it's me." I fully expected him to rush into my arms.

"Flint?" I tried again, looking more closely in case it was not him. No, it was definitely Flint, I recognised the defiant chin and blank stare, which grew blanker by the minute as I continued to call. He looked down at me nonchalantly, still clinging to Annie.

All the others came over to us, clambering up and giving an effusive welcome. William was as affectionate as ever and set about removing my hair clips and undoing my zip before going over to Stella. He fully gave the impression of being in charge and appeared to be reporting to Stella that all was well. After all, he had been in at the inception of the project and supervised the construction from the start.

Cheetah slapped my legs playfully and Pooh nestled to me in babyish repose. Flint and Annie continued to stand at a distance, holding each others' hands.

As we took them out of the enclosure, Tina swung down from a nearby tree. She was a large, almost mature female that had recently arrived and too independent to need to be confined. She had obviously only recently encountered mankind and remained wary although she was beginning to descend to take the occasional orange or banana and grasp a friendly outstretched hand. Albert, an older male, remained high up in the tree, as he was even more cautious and less tame. Albert had been missing for some months and not been seen in *Abuko*, until it seemed he had moved on elsewhere but had recently reappeared and 'given himself up' so to speak.

As we set out, Flint and Annie ran over to climb up me and Cheetah and William attempted to hitch a ride on my back. Stella told the larger ones to get down and walk, as they would certainly not still be carried by their mothers at that lanky stage.

“Hello Flinty.” I nuzzled him with my nose but he merely darted me a casual glance, without a glimmer of recognition.

“Look out, here comes Charlie!” Stella called back to us and the chimps all took to the trees and even Duffie, Stella’s dalmation dog, tried to scramble up.

I was watching out for at least a leopard or thought the Ninkey-nanker had materialised at last and paid no heed when a small antelope, an oribi, came running up, until I noticed his lowered head. As he charged towards me with his stumpy horns, Cheetah kindly lent me a hand and yanked me up into his tree and I realised why everybody had fled so hastily.

One by one the chimps ventured down, whilst Stella took Charlie back to the antelope enclosure. I looked for Flint, wondering what lofty height he had ascended to, as I heard his familiar helpless cries. I spotted him just as Annie was returning back up after him. She took his hand and lead him down safely from branch to branch, just the way Baba used to.

A larger antelope had joined us, a situtunga, who gazed around with gentle bovine eyes and twitching her glistening, black nose, following us on slender hooves. We wound our way along the path and stopped at the next fruiting tree; two humans, five young chimps, an antelope and a spotted dog. The two older chimps kept pace with the ill-assorted party moving through the trees. Just as they had once shared our environment, we were now privileged to share theirs.

I looked up at Flint, scrunching on a handful of wild figs more avaraciously than he had ever eaten fruit I had offered him indoors, William was grooming me, parting sections of my hair and Pooh snuggled up to Stella as she pointed out a fruiting branch. From the time Titan came into my life, I had dreamt of this virtual fantasia and now I was actually experiencing it.

It was not until my third visit that Flint showed any sign of recognition. It was after we had taken the chimps back into the enclosure and Flint was even helping himself to more than his fair share of the bananas that Stella was distributing and I ordered him to put them down. He turned towards me pouting, about to hoot at me in resentment, when suddenly his jaw dropped and he scrutinised my face in sudden recognition.

Having re-established himself with me, Flint gazed into my eyes searchingly (as apes have a tendency to do) leaving one with the distinct impression that they can see into one's very soul.

On subsequent visits to *Abuko* he would often revert to babyish traits, clinging to me for comfort, yet when with the other chimps, quite hold his own.

Squabbles often erupted, sparked off by a trivial cause and the melee could appear quite savage as they hurtled around. Hair bristling, faces snarling, the air was resonant with their supersonic screams. The rumpus would calm down again as suddenly as it had begun, the offended looking thwarted, would accept an apologetic hand, but the enmity soon forgotten, they would be romping together again.

By the time we were due to leave The Gambia, *Abuko* was really thriving and many orphans had moved in. It was becoming apparent as the chimps matured, that the time of such freedom they were enjoying would have to come to an end. Stella was planning to set up a rehabilitation site in Niokola Koba, a spacious Game Reserve in Senegal. She had been carrying out a vegetational survey which proved adequate to the chimps' needs and the area was already populated with wild chimpanzees.

For a time we became euphorical and wondered whether Titan might be able to join the group and I sought permission for his release from President Senghore himself. With his many affairs of state to attend to, the humane president/poet found time to consider the fate of one captive chimpanzee in his domain and readily agreed he could be released.

Alas, the folly of such a prospect gradually threatened the plan, as unfortunately, Titan, now fully mature, had greatly changed. For he was large and muscular, and apart from displaying signs of zoo neurosis, he was of truly titanic strength. He would obviously be even more unpredictable and although Stella was not concerned for her own welfare, others would at some time be at risk for he had lost all natural fear of man. We did not know whether he had any memory of other chimpanzees and his possible reaction to the youngsters was dubious to say the least. It was apparent that the entire project might well be in jeopardy should he join the rehabilitation group. I took comfort in the fact that all those who came after him would at least not experience his unhappy fate.

*   *   *   *   *   *   *   *

CHAPTER 12
TUBABOLU MORRISON MAKE DEY GO NEXT TOMORROW

I was loath to leave The Gambia as the time neared, for I considered myself fortunate to have lived in an unpressurised society and the remoteness had been almost like stepping back a century or two.

I had first realised that the 'wind of change' was beginning to waft across the peaceful Gambia when I narrowly escaped being attacked. I was walking the dogs along an ostensibly deserted beach one day when I became aware of a man running towards me wearing nothing but a smile. I soon twigged that he was not the Scandinavian tourist seeking directions that I had first assumed, as he appeared to be brandishing a knife! I took to my heels with an Olympian speed which I had been unaware I possessed, when suddenly Ebrima, my faithful stalker, burst out of the mangrove shrubs leaping towards the man. A frightening sight indeed! He was closely followed by several youths who had been studying for their imminent exams. They had been concealed in the tranquillity of the mangroves. They swiftly joined the chase pursuing the naked runner through the village to the taxi rank. We speculated how he would explain his unclothed state when he arrived in Banjul, the capital.

My gallant gang refused reward and I was delighted when I later learned that they had passed their exams and earned places at a Chinese University. As for Ebrima, he was worth his weight in scrounged ciggies! Later that day we learned that a tourist ship had docked in Banjul which explained the appearance of the 'stranger on the shore.'

It was obvious that 'civilization' was fast approaching! In the 1970's , The Gambia was being rudely ejected into the twentieth century, as the package tourists were arriving in force. The land of 'the next tomorrow' was fast disappearing, for the tourists were demanding services today.

Strange planes began to arrive on unscheduled days, which was most confusing when trying to gauge what day of the week it was. Previously it had been quite apparent by the bi-weekly BAC111. If it came in over the ocean it was Tuesday and a scramble to write outward mail, but if it flew out over the ocean it was Wednesday and too late to get letters off – not to worry, there was always the week after next week!

The developers had moved in and hotels sprang up along the expanse of palm-fringed beaches. It was unfortunate that they should have to be sandwiched between the various cemeteries of respective religions, as the dearly-departed citizens of the country already occupied the more scenic sites of the Costa del Sol Afrique, from Mile 1 almost to Mile 3.

By contrast to the colourful Gambian names of the villages, our unimaginative forbears had seen fit to name the ten mile stretch of coast from Banjul to the Cape, merely by mileage. I suppose it could be that the few who did manage to survive the White Man's Grave, were left with little inspiration or energy to do otherwise, due to the ravages of the climate and the many endemic fevers.

The hotel construction brought employment to many who had formerly had no concept of a working day and were most enthusiastic at the novelty of joining the ranks of the employed. The bulldozer, pile-driver and crane drivers became the new elite and regarded with an esteem previously reserved only for the *Alikalis* (Headmen) or *Imams*.

Crowds gathered to watch and cheer them as they enthusiastically mishandled the unfamiliar equipment – whoops, there goes another palm tree the Travel Agent might have preferred left in place! I was amused to be hailed by a familiar voice on a rooftop and recognised our local tree-climbing champion suitably re-employed. He had previously shinned up the palm trees to tap the nuts for oil.

Young Abdoullie had put a down-payment on a nifty French saloon car, having passed his driving test and joined the fleet of taxis that zoomed up and down the road. Moustafa's one-room dwelling on the corner, being situated in such a prominent site, he decided to send his sons fishing, his wife to deep fry with palm oil and erected a 'Fishes and Chipses' sign outside.

The design-as-you-go freehand machine embroiderists who had previously only embellished the Gambian *warrumbas* and kaftans in exchange for the promise of a chicken the next tomorrow or for service in kind, were beginning to relish the prospect of being paid in hard cash. Their skills were extended to new lines, batik and flour-sacking shirts, embroidered bags and bush hats – "we *savvy* dese people, dere 'eads not so strong for dee sun!" Holiday inscriptions would be machined on to some of the lavishly embroidered robes, almost as an afterthought, wishing the wearer, 'Good Luck', 'I Love You' and I once saw 'Kiss Me Quick'. Tailors soon surmised 'The Gambia' more appropriate to tourists' garb.

For centuries, the patterns had been passed down from the old laborious hand-embroiderers, they now flowed out mechanically on sophisticated electric sewing machines. The designer/machinist would pause to study his pattern, deciding on a kidney or heart shape, or maybe a liver or two, to fill in a suitable space. Their machines were now heard buzzing right through siesta and often well into the night, working whenever the power allowed. For electricity and water resources, never in adequate supply, were now strained by the additional needs of the hotels and frequently cut off.

Whilst sisters, wives and daughters were tying-and-dyeing in the back yard, their menfolk studied the latest copy of Vogue or even the unsolicited top-shelf magazines which arrived from Scandinavia. Ancient and modern motifs were wax printed and new traditions invented daily.

Everyone waited for the bonanza and pointed to the two new banks being built in our village alone, what more could one want as proof! 'Cheque Book', 'overdraft' and 'bank loan' crept into the vocabulary and any innovation was described as 'modern and nice' (modernised). Crowds gathered to gaze into the new air-conditioned supermarket as shelves were filled with luxury products everyone hoped would soon be within their reach.

The traditional deserving beggars, who had only sought alms on Jumo (Friday), now found it to their advantage to sit outside the new buildings every day of the week. Their numbers swelled and they were not all local, it was rumoured.

The more enterprising of the begging-letter writers extended their scope to multi-lingual requests, and producing a large assortment, would shuffle through, asking "Svensk? Dansk? Francais?" Having been most impressed with the African ability to master any new language, I was astounded with the ease and speed with which some of the youths had started to converse in obscure, guttural tongues. It was disappointing though to see so many bright school drop-outs, forsaking school desks to hang around the hotels.

Sleasy soul brothers materialised, donned in dark glasses and high-heeled boots. With their Afro-hairstyles and shoulder bags, they offered to show female visitors a good time. Nobody appeared to know them or from where they had come. Itinerant traders also drifted in from neighbouring states. Already shrewd merchants, they were not worried by the new Gambian small businessman, he would be no competition to them.

The occasional burglary was now heard of and for the first time people began to lock their doors. There had previously been only one competent house-breaker, which only necessitated being cautious during his infrequent and brief excursions out of Mile 2. 'Jail', 'pick-pocket' and 'mugger' were also newly-acquired words to creep into pidgin. There had always been chancers around the market but someone always yelled "t'ief-man" and everyone responded and rushed to tackle the rogue, who never got far.

A welcome was smiled to the sight-seeing strangers, as white faces looked in through the windows to see how the natives lived. Only recently they had welcomed and shared with the hippies that had strayed to their hospitable shores. They greeted the new globe-trotters with equally friendly welcome, particularly as their arrival augured something of a boon.

I watched with puzzled amusement, whilst visiting some friends in Bakau village one day. Some curious tourists loomed in the doorway and when my host threw a fez to the floor, everyone leapt up from their customary sprawling positions and proceeded to dance. After the onlookers had departed, obviously pleased with what they had seen, the occupants of the house flopped down again and I asked the reason for their spontaneous *hi-life*.

Everyone laughed and asked if I had not seen the latest brochure the travel agents were sending out. It apparently depicted The Gambia as a tropical paradise beyond all recognition and went so far as to say,

"The happy, smiling natives will jump up and dance at the drop of a hat!"

Naturist bathers now shared the beaches and swam in the sea where the old fishermen cast their nets. Sun-reddened buttocks polka-dotted the silver sands. I was struck by the incongruity of the early white missionaries, who had first come to preach to the heathen natives to cover their nakedness. It was now the lavishly-robed Africans who puzzled why their visitors chose to wear no clothes.

It was as if the slumbering, old Gambia had been woken after centuries of sleep by the fairy-tale, package-tour prince.

A subsequent wave of genealogical tourists were then yet to arrive. For following in Alex Haley's footsteps, many more were to be package-herded to the primitive land of ancestral roots. I was delighted to learn of Mr Haley's success in tracing his roots to my beloved Gambie Bolong. (Haley's Roots was a hugely successful book and television drama in the 1970's). I also found it an amusing coincidence that it should be in the very country where I had so recently discovered my own. For I came to the indubitable conclusion that my African lineage went back much further than Kunta Kinti. For Titan had convinced me within a few days of making his acquaintance, that he and I had a common ancestor that had swung through the same family tree.

Sangyang was already working for somebody else as a gardener and I asked them how he was getting on. They told me he was a very pleasant old man but the odd misunderstanding tended to occur. I was amazed when they told me he did not speak English, as I felt certain he did. I tried to recollect quite long conversations I was convinced we had held, but come to think of it, he had merely smiled his amiable smile and answered 'yes' and 'no'.

Landing decided to move into the hotel business and give some establishment the benefit of his *savoire-faire* – and I was certain the advantages of his superior services would render many a package-holiday the status of five-star.

On the day prior to our departure, a well-built young man with a pronounced nautical gait came sauntering into our compound. I did not recognise him until I opened the door and then there was no mistaking that broad, reassuring grin. Standing there with his hand outstretched was Mousa N'dow from the 'Ladywright' whom we had only seen once more after we had Titan.

"Mousa! How good to see you. You only just came in time as we are leaving The Gambia tomorrow." But the talking drums had conveyed the message.

"I *savvy* dat, so make I come tell you goodbye".

I deemed it something of a compliment, as although Mousa regularly traversed the country by boat, when he accompanied us home with Titan, it had been the first time he had made the ten mile journey from Banjul to Cape. Like many others who had been born and lived in the capital, they never had reason to trek out to the westerly point and lived and died without ever crossing Denton Bridge.

"What have you been doing? Did you sign on with a ship and see the world as you hoped?"

"Na". He hung his head, smiling coyly. "I stay for The Gambia but now I reach Captain." He visibly swelled, holding his head erect.

"Captain!" I exclaimed, "what's the name of your vessel?"

"I be the master for the Farafenny Ferry now" he proudly announced.

It certainly explained the mystery of when our neighbour Kebba Foon had returned from an up-country campaign, saying that the ferryman expressly sent his greetings to us. We had not been aware of any up-country ferryman that knew us.

It seemed that the reliable Gambian bush telegraph had conveyed the news of our departure right up the slender vein of the country equally promptly, and probably more efficiently than conventional communication. One never discovered the means by which news travelled and it was not too wild a stretch of the imagination to believe that the talking drum relayed a regular six o'clock news, '*Tubabolu* (Europeans) Morrisons make dey go next tomorrow'.

Mousa had also heard the news that Titan had gone to *Dakar* after all and had visited him in Hann Park and taken him some bananas, as had many of his other Gambian friends. I was about to go out to *Abuko* just as Mousa arrived, so it was fitting that he should join me and meet all the new chimpanzees. Being a fellow chimpomaniac he was delighted with all that he saw, as right from the meeting with Titan, he had felt that he should have had such an opportunity. Having come full circle, it was less heart-breaking having to say goodbye to Flint, knowing he would never be encloistered in a zoo. And all the residents had been able to stay in Africa.

The Brewers' house was growing, adjacent to *Abuko* Reserve and just as I had at first envisaged, conveniently close to their ever-extending wildlife family. Eddie had retired from Forestry and the Government set up a Conservation Department, which he was to so deservedly become director of, and they were building him a suitable home.

We left from the intimate, old airport, but a modern, international terminal was already under construction. Grossly laden with hand luggage, with possessions we had not thought to send on ahead, we were further burdened with much-appreciated but cumbersome gifts, some of which would be unsuitable to take on board the plane. Fish, fruit and several live chickens, not to mention a prize pumpkin which must have weighed all of 40 pounds. I felt most discourteous declining and the reasons difficult to explain. The grower was most crestfallen and thought the only problem was placing it on my head, and produced a coil of plaited raffia to cushion it upon.

The plane was delayed long after we had boarded as the airline officials came on board to count and re-count heads It at least gave a late-arriving well-wisher time to nip through the barrier and come on board to bid us farewell, in typically casual Gambian style. After studying the passenger list and conferring with the crew, the discrepancy did not appear to have been cleared but with a last familiar Gambian shoulder-shrug, the plane was sent off on its way.

However, I was not prepared for my last sight of The Gambia to be so spectacular. As I looked down at Cape Point, it was a colourful mosaic of people looking up and waving. Several people had expressed their intention of coming to the airport but I had dissuaded them, as I knew I would be even more emotional. Not to be outdone, even by a Hollywood spectacular, it appeared that half the village had turned out. I felt so special realising my fellow passengers looking down had no idea the crowd scene was just for me.

I changed out of the light cotton, embroidered outfit a local friend had kindly made for a surprise, to wear on the journey, stipulating

"Make you wear vesty underside – maybe London too much cold."

I would have somehow felt ostentatious arriving at Gatwick on a dreary November night, dressed in exotic costume, carrying live chickens, a large barracuda, a hand of bananas with a giant pumpkin perched upon my head - albeit wearing a vest!

EPILOGUE
REHABILITATION

Stella was to spend the remainder of her life devoted to the rehabilitation of chimps. Still in her teens at first, she took a few to live out in the bush, teaching them the rudiments of survival in a natural habitat.

Today, over 30 years later, there are over 90 surviving on an up-river island in The Gambia. Apart from food supplement and monitoring their wellbeing, they live independent lives within structured social groups. Otherwise they would most likely have been transported to Europe for zoos, photographers or worse, laboratories, whilst a large proportion probably would not have survived the voyage. It appeared to us a latter-day slave trade of our closest relatives.

On my return back to the UK, I desperately missed my contact with the chimps. I became a regular visitor at London Zoo and Twycross Zoo, particularly when they were both sending a pair of chimps for rehabilitation. I regularly visited Yula and Cameron at Regents Park, joyfully anticipating the freedom they were about to experience. I told them about the jungle and their new family. I am sure they understood, as I speak fluent chimpanzee! I also visited Monty whilst he was at Dudley Zoo. His face had darkened as he was a mature, adult male, but he remained his sweet-natured, docile self and he appeared to remember me.

I constantly awaited the post for the detailed news Stella regularly sent of my erstwhile hairy friends. When she visited, our conversation must have sounded as if we discussed some sensational TV soap.

"Does William still look up ladies' skirts?"

"Have you found out who got Tina pregnant?"

"Does Annie still smoke? She didn't start until she was two."

Stella had been commissioned to write a book, which I very much enjoyed helping her with. It was good to re-live our shared memories. We could get quite transported, sitting at my dining table, back to Africa. On one occasion, delivering rather realistic hyena howls, searching for a description, we became aware of the disconcerted face of a delivery man at the window. I guess there are not too many hyenas in rural Kent!

On one visit, Stella had a call from her father telling her that Happy (who was a particularly handsome lad) had lost his eyesight due to diabetes. We were heartbroken that one of the few chimps who had a chance to live a life of freedom, would now need to be confined for his own safety.

Doug and I were then posted to Malawi – a beautiful, scenic country: a tropical Scotland, with wonderful, friendly people – yet not an ape to be seen! Doug hoped I might like to get acquainted with baboons or the vervet monkeys, but I realised I had become a primate snob! There were rumours of a lone chimpanzee often sighted up-country; I pursued this hopefully but came to the conclusion it was of the same species as the Ninky-Nanker or even the Yeti! At the same time, I was only too aware that Jane Goodall was studying wild chimps in neighbouring Tanzania.

I longed to escape back to bush freedom and away from Malawian restrictions. Censored newspapers and movies, knee length skirts and shorts and female slacks a prisonable offence – even a kilt. Ladies glided around the supermarket wearing floor-length skirts, appearing to be going on to some function. It was also an offence to grow hair below the ears (that is the men of course).

I had to go through quite a rigmarole with a panel of censors before my wildlife paintings were allowed to go on exhibition. It all depended whether they were real, living animals! I said they were fictitious, which appeared to render them respectable. Azungus (ex-pats) rarely got out of their cars and would blast on their horns for their gardeners to open the compound gate. I felt conspicuous if I so much as walked the dog around the block. The house and telephone were bugged and people were inclined to hold private conversations only in their cars.

When the French Embassy put on my art exhibition, there was a lengthy Africanesque eulogy about me on the radio. I listened in frozen terror, expecting the Police to burst in – people had been jailed or deported for far less. I am pleased to say it must have gone unreported. It was so very different from those 'cool', flower-power days in laid-back Gambia.

At this time, Stella had established her camp in Niokola Koba National Park in neighbouring Senegal with several of her chimps, as well as others. On leaving Malawi, I flew straight back to West Africa, over the chimp and gorilla belts at last. I hitched a lift from up-country Gambia to the nearest small town to the park, Tambakounda. On being hauled up onto the groundnut lorry, I was intrigued by the reddish complexion of fellow passengers, which I took to be distinctive of some unfamiliar tribe. However, on making our first 'comfort' stop (ladies to the bushes on the nearside, gents to the off, (African fashion) I discovered that I too was a shade of raw umber with titian hair! It was the dust off the laterite road surface. I therefore swathed my towel over my face fully yashmacked, save for my red panda eyes. I reported to Military HQ on arrival, as instructed, which felt rather formal. I was offered a shower (which tends to be the first gesture of African hospitality) and joined the officers for a scrumptious lunch.

I was then transported on a large military vehicle, heading a convoy of troops. Whilst privileged to sit in the front alongside a gold-braided, medal-infested gentleman, my seat was awkwardly positioned. My legs being adjacent to the gear-lever, I had to move them from one side to the other each time the driver changed gear, depending on whether he was shifting up or down. My feet felt as if I was resting them on red-hot coals from the inferno produced by the engine. The air temperature must have been 120 degrees or more - I felt no need of a hot water bottle for my tootsies! My feet and ankles were visibly ballooning up, my lips swollen and parched and I appeared to have lost all sensation in my tongue. Mon Capitaine was extremely popular and cheered and waved at by the crowds who thronged the roadside along our route. I assumed that he must be a local conquering hero.

We occasionally stopped at villages, where people rushed to shake his hand. Our *'Soldat Célèbre'* would stand saluting as ladies flocked to offer him bowls of the most mouth-drooling, thirst-quenching water, wetter than any I had ever seen! He took prodigious gulps with appreciative gallic lip smacks, somewhat tormentingly towards me, his thirsty companion, I felt. It was so surreal, I felt as if I was performing in a French Foreign Legion movie or even a Jaques Tati farce.

I had not the least idea of where I was being taken, except I would have to hitch a further distance to Stella's camp from wherever I was dropped. I tried not to dwell on tales of the white slave trade and to retain an enigmatic composure, normally reserved for the London Underground.

I was most relieved when we did stop and I was off-loaded at a Rest Lodge, deep in the bush. My French being that of the school-girl variety, I gleaned *'Chef d'État'* so it must be President Senghore's rural retreat – marvellous! Only as the sound of the trucks subsided in the distance did I feel a sense of abandonment. From the little I had managed to understand, I gathered I must wait for a vehicle going in Stella's direction, but with much French shoulder-shrugging, gathered there were no visitors as the Reserve was closed in the rainy season. I had heard 'jour' and 'semaine' – did this mean I might wait days or even weeks? I just hoped that the large quantity of egg and tomato sandwiches that Eddie Brewer had made for me would last!

The ramshackle wooden chalet ravaged by weather and white ant left me speculating on the insalubrious conditions African Presidents endured, recalling the cabin on the Ladywright. Although I guess I can boast of having slept in the beds of Presidents!

I had rather hoped there might have been a 'concierge' waiting to run me a bubble bath and rustle up some delicious supper. The dwelling had been abandoned, unlocked but I doubted that even squatters would have considered it a 'des res'.

There was no fear of intruders as had occurred in Tamba Kounda where I was offered an unoccupied company house in the heart of the town. People were rattling at the door the entire night and I had to move heavy furniture against it to prevent entry. I concluded that some trusted employee was subsidising his wages, renting it out by the hour. I doubted there would be many ladies of the night out in the sticks.

I then experienced a night in which one's hair would be expected to turn instantly white. As dusk fell, I discovered I was far from alone. There were scufflings, scrunchings and scamperings galore – and having checked the bed for venomous sleeping partners, I curled up under the illusionary safety of the moth-eaten mosquito nets. Fortunately, I am blessed with a primitive escape mechanism, an ability to fall into a deep, instant sleep when faced with an intolerable situation, such as being scared witless! I was therefore rendered oblivious of any further nocturnal activity.

I paced the roadside for most of the next day, my sandwiches long-since devoured. By late afternoon, I was fully resigned to a further night from hell. Then I heard the distinctive, welcome sound of an approaching Land Rover, throbbing towards me. It was occupied by two pediatric doctors travelling to a monthly clinic they ran, which was very fortuitous for me. Did I mention I also have this very useful guardian angel?

Never had I been so pleased to see a familiar face as when Stella ran out to greet me. The cacophony of a hooting and squealing welcome from the chimps was music to my ears! I instantly felt I had come home to a former primaeval paradise.

Stella had constructed a modest two-roomed building, the kitchen being outside (viz the camp fire), the bathroom was situated down in the valley, consisting of a pool damned up from a mountain stream of clear, soft water. By merely removing one stone, the plug was pulled out. The loo was 100 metres from camp in any direction.

I only had a day to get into a routine as Stella had to go to *Dakar*. I was left in very capable hands, those of Renee and Edirisa, who both continue to be dedicated to the project. The haute-cuisine was of a very high standard, but only when the store-cupboard permitted – more often than not, stocks tended to run out. At such times we resorted to a staple diet of rice and tomato sauce but would fantasise that it was Beef Wellington or coq au vin (or even fish and chips) which did somehow enhance the taste. This was supplemented by the fruit and nuts we gathered on our daily treks, which was doubtlessly a healthy diet. We always bathed and dressed for dinner which complemented the imaginary menu.

I devised a sweet/sour sauce with vinegar, tomato sauce and local honey. If we caught the tiniest fish, it appeared to be a feast – but a morsel always to be left for the following days' bait. More than once we caught a teeny crocodile, but resisted having it for Sunday lunch.

Each morning was spent out with our band of rascals to teach them to forage. We would point out fruiting trees, termite mounds and show them how to crack open large *baobab nuts* with a rock. After a short distance, they would whimper and hold their arms up to be carried, much as toddlers do. Although it was possible to convey three or four (one front, one back and one on each hip), their mothers would not have continued to carry them.

We would return at midday and whilst Stella wrote up her log, I reclined in the hammock with chimps clambering over me and I would fall asleep with them grooming me – bliss!

There were still plenty of nocturnal munchings and scrunchings, but at least from the safety of the other side of the wall, leaving us to conject what manner of beast it might be. The need to get up for the loo during the night called for a sense of adventure. One first had to bang on top of the door on opening it, when assorted snakes would shower down. Picking one's way cautiously in the dark to the snaps and crackles (and even pops!) as unidentified creatures retreated into the undergrowth. The reward for a nocturnal tinkle was a caravan of elephants seemingly gliding as they silently browsed through the trees. Only the snapping of branches betrayed their presence. The fact that I was able to view them from the safety of the opposite bank of a very large, deep ravine was a distinct advantage. I admit to being rather scared of elephants, especially when they charge trumpeting through raised trunks. Stella had wanted us to sleep in the treetops with the chimps, like proper chimp mums, but I did not fancy being rudely awakened and hurled out of bed by an intruding trunk!

Days ran into weeks until it became difficult to keep track of time, except for when the bi-weekly plane from *Dakar* flew over. Stella's only contact with the outside world in an emergency was when she could place an SOS on her roof. I had not previously appreciated the extent of her isolation, especially in the rainy season. I was in awe of her trail-blazing courage. She had experienced many traumas and dangers, but the only wildlife she feared were the bees. For not only were they of the aggressive African strain, but she experienced a violent allergic reaction to them. I had arrived bearing a flagon of fragrant cologne, guaranteed to attract bees, I realised tinned meat would have been a more acceptable gift. Silly me! On one occasion there, I was bitten on the foot by a snake, which swished off before I could identify it. Renee, the camp assistant did nothing to reassure me when he more or less implied that we would not know if it was venomous or not depending upon whether I survived the night! Pleased to say, I did! Another evening I had been enjoying a relaxing bath in the pool, whilst the chimps gathered around trying to pinch the precious soap. It was only after I'd dried and dressed that I looked up and discovered a pair of topaz eyes watching me – those of a breathtakingly beautiful leopard, languishing on an overhead branch; the one and only time I ever saw one in the wild. I endeavoured to make a slow, calm exit, belying my mounting panic, ushering the chimps ahead of me, more concerned for their safety. Fortunately, the exotic pussy must have already had his dinner!

Living in such a wild and natural environment, one's senses soon become heightened, particularly that of hearing. One day, the silence was shattered by the approaching roar of what sounded like a convoy of heavy-duty vehicles. We hoped it was only passing by.

It was indeed a convoy, a fleet of French Army vehicles, out on manoeuvres. The sudden intrusion after a time of prolonged isolation was quite traumatic. Social graces forgotten, we became quite tongue-tied, stereotyping the couple of cave-women they obviously perceived us to be. We did, however, fetch them drinking water from the stream. They had at first been amazed to discover two wild women living with a tribe of apes! We were not sorry to see them go as they had delighted in teasing the chimps, which could well have ended in tears, although the tins of meat we managed to scrounge from them were a rare treat. I have since bought the same brand, recalling how delicious it was, only to disappointedly end up having to give it to the dog. There is nothing like starvation to refine the palate.

The next occasion when we heard an approaching vehicle was indeed a welcome visitor: Stella's father Eddie. We leapt around like a couple of excited chimps and gave him huge hugs. It really was not just for the tins of corned beef and baked beans he brought. He had also collected post, as Stella awaited some important letters, but there was only the one and that was for me. My Auntie Flossie, an intrepid correspondent, had written to tell me that the washing had failed to dry on Monday and the Sunday joint had tasted off! I commented that she would reach me even in Timbuktu, only to realise we were, in fact, only a mere stone's throw away.

Eddie had continued to develop the nature reserve, *Abuko*, often financed from his own pocket and working tirelessly for his orphans, including once a litter of hand-reared hyenas. He could rarely be persuaded to take leave, to the extent that he did not manage to get to the Palace to receive his OBE (thereafter referred to as 'Old Blue Eyes'). He received international acclaim when he pursued and recovered a stolen chimp in Austria and like a true hero, broke up a 'chimp-nap' ring.

At the time of the abortive coup, he had taken to the bush on seeing vehicles enter the compound and for some days had survived on nuts and berries, in true Tarzan fashion. This was long after his official retirement, when he had naturally stayed on.

As tourism grew, *Abuko* became a great attraction and but for Eddie, no conservation would have existed. Bwana Brewer was guaranteed to enliven an uneventful conducted tour.

"Keep still...." he would stage whisper, "...something is breaking cover." He was so convincing that visitors would attest to having seen a leopard themselves. Even I could imagine I had.

Never one to seek acclaim, his fame spread and he was recognised by wildlife luminaries worldwide, until one never knew who one might bump into in 'l'le ol' *Abuko*'. I once discovered a rather agitated American lady who was endeavouring to recover her camera from William, already having been subjected to the knicker inspection. I gradually realised it was the American Envoy to Ghana who was formerly known as Shirley Temple, the Hollywood child star. She had broken her journey to venture into the interior at dusk, which not many people would brave. She took all of Will's pranks in such good humour, I warmed to the lady. Despite becoming a respected figure in the wildlife fraternity, Eddie remained the same unassuming, humourous boy from Lewisham, as he referred to himself.

I once arrived on a visit to be puzzled by the identity of his departing guest, as his voice was so familiar. It was only when he said he had to get back for the National, I realised it was Raymond Glendenning, a well-known sports commentator. Eddie had experienced a succession of exalted visitors and greeted me,

"You don't know how good it is to have you here, someone you can fart with!" To this day, the greatest compliment I was ever paid!

He also had a phenomenal memory for recitation and would burst into 'The Charge of the Light Brigade' at any time. Many was the nonsense poem he inspired me to write, such as 'There's a blue-eyed fella idle to the west of Llandudno'.

It was incongruous to see him in North Wales after he was forced to retire due to his ageing bones. He appeared a fish out of water, a veritable Crocodile Dundee. The Welsh appeared confounded by him, especially when he would burst into one of his epic poems at inappropriate times.

Another of his animal-loving admirers was the film star Brigitte Bardot. She sent him fan letters regularly and I would find myself having to nag him to reply to her but doubt he ever did. I visited him ostensibly in an endeavour to extract his memoirs out of him, but alas, his interesting life was never recorded for posterity. He was also a brilliant photographer of wildlife and try as I may, high quality slides remained uncatalogued. Invariably his enthusiasm had become diverted to his newly-found culinary pursuits, such as lobscouse stew or writing names in icing sugar for guests on the instant custard he had so dedicatedly whipped up. I felt so privileged to have known such a remarkable man – particularly as he appeared to prefer my company to that of silver-screen sirens.

His daughters, Heather and Stella were equally remarkable and followed in their father's footsteps, Heather having founded The Gambian Horse and Donkey Trust. Like Stella, she too had set up educational programmes and medical care, also creating employment.

My wilderness idyll that was Niokola Koba Reserve passed only too soon and I was most reluctant to return to civilisation. It was as if Tina (the semi-wild chimp) realised I was leaving. On my last day, she made one of her rare visits into camp with Tilly, her baby, whom we had seen little of. She came over close to me, gently placing a hand on my arm whilst I proffered the back of my hand in polite chimp acknowledgement. To my utter amazement and delight, she relinquished her hold on Tilly, who clambered onto my leg and proceeded to climb up me into my arms. Thrilled as I was, I felt uncertain how much contact she would allow me with her daughter, but she continued to encourage her offspring to get acquainted with an auntie. I finally handed her back to her mother, thanking Tina profusely. I have never been more honoured, except perhaps the time I met the great ape himself – Guy the Gorilla – but that's another story.

Stella continued with the rehabilitation programme for over thirty years. When her husband, David retired, they sold up their home and moved permanently to Chimpsville. David built a platformed camp on stilts over the River Gambia, a sort of super-decking. They provided a tented rest camp where visitors could stay to view, not only the chimps, but the prolific bird-life, hippos and even the odd manatee on their own holiday doorstep. The Trust is currently being administered by an American naturalist with funding from the Friends of Animals Charity in the United States, allegedly in collaboration with the Gambian Government.

Whilst fundraising continued to be limited, Stella was gaining recognition and in 2007 not only did she go to the Palace for her OBE, but was presented with an honorary degree at Glasgow University. Tragically, she was soon afterwards diagnosed with cancer which we all fully thought she would conquer with her usual determination, but sadly she passed away early in 2008. At her request, she was buried near chimp island with her beloved chimpanzees. Her motto had always been 'They said it couldn't be done and so I went and did it!'

THE END

GLOSSARY OF TERMS

'Abuko'	Nature Reserve established by Eddie Brewer in The Gambia
'ad nauseum'	Endless
'Alikali'	Headman of the village
'baobab nuts'	Fruit of large African tree
'Chef d'État'	Chief of State
'chop'	Pidgin for 'food'
'Dakar	Capital of Sengal
'fo'c'sle'	The front of the boat
'humbug'	Pidgin for annoy, pester.
'dashed'	Pidgin for bribed
'Galagoes'	Species of bushbaby
'Gmlina'	Indigenous Gambian tree
'hi-life'	West African dance
'jobo'	Mandinka for parrot
'ju-jus'	Amulets and charms of West Africa
'jumbukaturri'	Local medicine
'Kangkarangs'	Groups of dancing and singing youths
'Kola'	Addictive African nut

'koriteh'	Muslim feast
'Ikoo'	Mandinka for 'pardon?'
'Imam'	Head of the Mosque
'Mandinka'	Local language of The Gambia
'Mungo Park'	African pioneer
'ndemo'	Mandinka for chimpanzee
'piccan'	Pidgin for 'youngster'
'palaver'	Bother/trouble
'Ramadan'	Muslim fast
'Soldat Célèbre'	Distinguished soldier
'tiko'	Head-dress
'tubabolu'	Mandinka for 'European people'
'warrumba'	Loose African robe (like a kaftan)
'Wolof'	Tribe in Sene-Gambia
'Yundum'	A village in The Gambia